THEME OF THE VOLUME

For those who have suffered failure or defeat, be patient toward all that is unsolved. Do not now seek the answers that cannot be given to you because you would not be able to live them. Respond to the questions of life by answering for your life; perhaps, then, you will gradually, and without noticing it, live into the answer.

From Lawyer to Warrior

FROM
LAWYER

TO
WARRIOR

*Failing the Bar, Becoming a Marine,
and Finding Meaning*

CHRIS PAVLAK

HOUNDSTOOTH
PRESS

FROM LAWYER TO WARRIOR
Failing the Bar, Becoming a Marine, and Finding Meaning

FIRST EDITION

ISBN   978-1-5445-3845-7 *Hardcover*
       978-1-5445-3846-4 *Paperback*
       978-1-5445-3847-1 *Ebook*

Dedicated to
those who have failed:
Brian Christopher Grauman
April 30, 1992–November 18, 2016
those who have fallen:
Sergeant Ian M. Tawney, USMC
December 3, 1984–October 16, 2010
and, to St. Jude
the Patron Saint of Hopeless and Impossible Causes

CONTENTS

Defeat

Defeat, my Defeat, my solitude and my aloofness;
You are dearer to me than a thousand triumphs,
And sweeter to my heart than all world-glory.
Defeat, my Defeat, my self-knowledge and my defiance,
Through you I know that I am yet young and swift of foot
And not to be trapped by withering laurels.
And in you I have found aloneness
And the joy of being shunned and scorned.
Defeat, my Defeat, my shining sword and shield,
In your eyes I have read
That to be enthroned is to be enslaved,
And to be understood is to be leveled down,
And to be grasped is but to reach one's fullness
And like a ripe fruit to fall and be consumed.
Defeat, my Defeat, my bold companion,
You shall hear my songs and my cries and my silences,
And none but you shall speak to me of the beating of wings,
And urging of seas,
And of mountains that burn in the night,
And you alone shall climb my steep and rocky soul.
Defeat, my Defeat, my deathless courage,
You and I shall laugh together with the storm,
And together we shall dig graves for all that die in us,
And we shall stand in the sun with a will,
And we shall be dangerous.

BY KAHLIL GIBRAN

FOREWORD

Carlton W. Kent,
16th Sergeant Major of the Marine Corps

The proudest moments of my life as a Marine are the day I earned the title of United States Marine, the day I became a non-commissioned officer; and serving with thousands and thousands of Marines over my career, especially warriors in combat. In these moments—as in all moments of life—I believe that where I am, whom I am with, and the events that unfold are in the hands of Providence. Things happen for a reason even though I might not know how or why.

One of the most meaningful days in my thirty-six-year career was on November 8, 2004, as the I Marine Expeditionary Force (I MEF) Sergeant Major. At the height of the conflict in Iraq and conditions having been set for I MEF's assault on the city of Fallujah to engage in the most kinetic urban combat since Hue City, Vietnam, I witnessed eye-watering events as warriors pushed into the city. The fighting was tough, and the city came at a high cost. But persevering through adverse conditions and maintaining a warfighting spirit are the hallmarks of every Marine; it is the reason why people join the Marine Corps.

The hands of Providence connected me to Chris Pavlak through my son-in-law, Tony Bates. Tony and Chris attended the Basic School, where they were in the same platoon, Infantry Officer Course, and Ground Intelligence Officer Course. When both were assigned to Camp Pendleton, California, they became roommates and very close friends. During a recent visit to Camp LeJeune, North Carolina, I was speaking with my son-in-law about his perseverance because he is the epitome of the word "persevere." Tony was severely wounded during combat operations in Afghanistan on June 26, 2011. His combat injuries resulted in the amputation of his leg and he suffered other combat injuries from the improvised explosive device. Nevertheless, Tony volunteered to continue serving on active duty and he still does today. During our conversation, Tony spoke with me about Chris and his own story of perseverance.

After hearing Chris's story, I knew it was important for him to tell his story to the world because everyone has experienced struggles, setbacks, and failures. His personal story is of failing the Bar exam several times, becoming a Marine and, after his transition from active duty, finding himself in a situation wondering how he would put food on his table. His story would be an inspiration for others who are going through similar struggles.

Failure is considered a taboo that no one talks about. One attribute that quickly evaporates amid today's social media posts and pictures is authenticity. Chris's story of coming up short again and again, but finding meaning through it all, is anything but inauthentic.

After the enormous amount of work of law school, then sitting for the Bar exam and never passing, he revectored himself to become a U.S. Marine. When we met in August, he told me that he first began to write this book to capture the impact that earning the title of United States Marine and graduating from Infantry Officer Course in June 2008 had on his life. After my thirty-six years of active duty service in the Marine Corps, I truly understood the importance of such events. But as he continued writing, Chris wanted to share his story with others who may be going through similar experiences. As a Marine and servant-leader, he decided to take point and help others navigate their own failures and setbacks by offering a story of resilience to those who think they may be at their own devastating dead end.

As Providence would have it, once again, I am crossing the line of departure with a fellow warrior as he attempts to gain a foothold on a narrative and shape the battlespace from the chaos of failure into perseverance, resilience, meaning, and hope. I strongly recommend this book to all readers to gain an understanding that a person is not alone in their struggles, to stay strong in your faith and never let failures keep you from your destiny.

INTRODUCTION

*"God, whose law it is that he who learns must suffer; and even in
our sleep, pain that cannot forget falls drop by drop upon the heart.
And in our own despite, against our will, comes wisdom to us by
the awful grace of God."*

—Aeschylus

In October 2006 and February 2007, I received news that would
forever change my life. I had failed the Minnesota Bar Exam
twice in a row. Outwardly, it meant I would not be taking the
oath to be an attorney, would not practice law, and would not be
starting my career. Underneath those superficialities, however,
lay ugly insecurities that, until that point, I had not realized I
had harbored—intense feelings of inadequacy and hopelessness
began to emerge. I had been so deeply immersed in law school's
toxic environment I did not realize who I had become: an academic narcissist—a person who was hyper-vigilant about status,
fixated on financial ascendancy, and insistent on comparing
myself to others. When chaos reared its ugly head in the form of
failing the Bar, those dangerous emotions I had been ignoring
abruptly metastasized into self-deprecation, inadequacy, and

hopelessness. I had done everything in my power to prevent the possibility of failure from occurring, but now terrifying prospects of an unknown world were staring me in the face.

In the days and weeks that followed, and through a fog of messy emotions, I continued trying to make sense of what had happened—what was happening—and I obsessively mulled the particulars of what I might have done wrong. I replayed over and over in my head the details of the exams, how much I had studied, and how assiduously I had worked the previous three years in law school. I had just squandered the last ten months of my life going nowhere. Worse still was the fact that I was in a professional limbo—not a student and not a lawyer. I faced the horrible prospect of studying for the Bar yet again for a third time and then anxiously awaiting the results. The comfortable, predictable, and optimistic present had vanished.

Grief gave way to anguish as the vision of my ideal self as a practicing attorney and the financial ascendancy I so badly desired faded from view only to be replaced by joblessness, self-doubt, staggering debt, and insecurity. Failure was not supposed to be part of my reality, and now it had implications across several aspects of my life. I had to recalibrate my goals. As I peered into my unknown future, I searched for direction amidst an otherwise rudderless life.

As I considered the sunk costs of law school—financial and temporal—I thought there was no way to change course. I went to law school to live the life of an attorney, which I thought I wanted, driven completely by my own short-sighted ego. But, imperceptibly, during my three years of law school, *life was shaping me* and was pushing back onto me in the form of measuring myself by external validation, schadenfreude (pleasure derived from another's misfortune), and academic narcissism. I identified only with status and material gain. I thought (incorrectly) the only way to shape my future was to increase its material and pecuniary scale and scope so I might have the life I thought I wanted.

Whenever a difficult and worthwhile pursuit is undertaken, an ethic emerges. If a goal is valuable, sacrifices are made to achieve it, delaying gratification. The ethic manifests such that the individual seeking the goal feels he is worth it or has earned it because he has sacrificed so many other things in pursuit of it. However, repeatedly failing to achieve it can skew how one perceives himself and thus turn on its head the belief that hard work does eventually pay off.

Before failing, I had already adopted such an ethic and had told myself becoming an attorney was a worthy pursuit—worth the three years of hard work, sacrifice, and tens of thousands of dollars of debt. But my repeated inability to attain the goal resulted in a personal encounter with something terrible and unknown. It remained invisible to others and for some time, remained hidden to me. It spread like a cancer as it infected the thoughts, ideas, and beliefs I had of myself and my own abilities. It metastasized into an insidious problem. The cancerous thoughts attached themselves to otherwise normal errors or shortcomings, but unmercifully and exponentially magnified their significance. It was toxic shame, and I found myself in the swampland of the soul unable to forgive myself for my failures.

In writing this book, I have learned that suicide is disturbingly common among recent law school graduates who subsequently fail the Bar exam. In 2013, a twenty-six-year-old accomplished and well-liked student from Drexel University's Earle Mack School of Law had failed the Bar exam twice. He committed suicide a few days before he was to begin preparing for his third attempt. In 2016, another charismatic and well-liked student from the University of California Hastings School of Law unfortunately failed the July 2016 California Bar Exam and also took his own life in November of that year.

I have failed the Bar exam four times and have never passed it. Each failure rocked my life to its core. In my search for answers, I had been unable to find any book or person who might be able to empathize with what I was going through. I was looking for someone who had been here before to tell me, "I know what you are feeling. I know it is excruciating. And I know there are no answers right now, but find something to strive for, something to pursue. Find purpose. And you are going to be OK." If I was going to stop the downward spiral, I somehow had to reshape my life.

This book is not an indictment of the practice of law. It is one person's experience of a contemporary American third-tier law school and the devastating effects of failing the Bar exam. That experience was one of extreme competition, hyper-vigilance of academic performance, and seeking external validation from the industry I wanted so badly to enter. It is simply an unvarnished look at the process of becoming an attorney, the effects of failure, and the resilience to reshape one's life.

The incredibly devastating and self-loathing defeat of failure left me struggling to make sense of it. I realized I could either shrink from fear of the unknown and wallow in the pain or forge a new trail. Moreover, lacking faith in my abilities or harboring a fear of the unknown would simultaneously prevent me from finding any meaning in my suffering. Instead, it turned out, *my* fulfillment lay in the potential to find meaning in the uniqueness of *my own* personal tragedy.

What I sought was the knowledge that I was not merely the sum of the terrible emotions that were occupying my mind, and that I could, yet, add something to this equation to yield a positive result. My vulnerability presented experiential, creative, and attitudinal values with which I would have to reshape my life. I had to consider that these failures themselves might be where I find the answer. What I sought and what I'm sure the two students mentioned above sought was meaning. In order to find meaning, I would have to risk being alone, open, and vulnerable to the nature of reality, and confront the unknown world that exists on the other side of failure.

During law school, I had considered the Marine Corps in the hopes of becoming a Staff Judge Advocate—a military lawyer. Not only was this option closed off to me because I could not pass the Bar, but I had learned that due to an influx in the number of men and women who had already accepted a law contract with the Marine Corps, there were no more law contracts for my recruiting region. So, I had a decision to make. I could walk away from the Marine Corps and continue to try and pass the Bar exam—not knowing when or if I would ever pass. Or I could join the Marine Corps as a ground contract and enter into the unknown, unsure where the future may lead. With my back up against the wall, I chose the second alternative. All I had was hope that I might be able to somehow move forward and, more importantly, find meaning in my failures.

That meaning, or at least the beginning of it, would come eighteen months later, the day I graduated from the United States Marine Corps Infantry Officer Course.

As I considered how these failures led to my service in the Marine Corps and how they forever positively changed the trajectory of my life, when I returned from a deployment to Afghanistan in 2020, I wanted to share my story with others who have failed—not only the Bar exam, but any significant undertaking—anything one has spent weeks, months, or years preparing for, striving for, and working towards that ends in loss, failure, or catastrophe. This book is for those whose lives might be immobilized in a nadir of shame, loss, and humiliation like mine was. I wanted to share something I have only learned through failing, something I wish I would have known at the time I was at my lowest: *that failure is an opportunity to willfully and courageously confront the chaos of life and creatively explore the unknown. It is a chance to relinquish false narratives of success and realize narratives of excellence by responding to life's questions in the affirmative—seeking to live up to one's potential in spite of setbacks.* While I agree that readers are often poorly served when an author writes as an act of catharsis, I felt compelled to make sense of my failures. I hoped meaning might be found by spilling my soul about my misguided financial ambitions of being an attorney, the humiliation and shame of failing the Bar exam four times, and how I overcame those failures—that meaning might be found in exploring the opportunities failure presented. This book is the fruit of that compulsion.

In the tumultuous upheaval of my life's ambitions, I learned that only when a person transforms his interior life can he begin the process of mining the experience to discover the meaning in it. Each time I failed the Bar exam I had to confront chaos I felt might envelop me. Each time I was forced to explore the unknown and move in what I thought was a positive direction. Only in this exploration would I be able to respond to these questions of life by answering *for* my life, so that one day I might become worthy of my failures.

PART I

DEFEAT

Chapter 1

———

THE CALL TO
ADVENTURE

*"Having an adventure shows that someone is incompetent, that
something has gone wrong. An adventure is interesting enough
in retrospect, especially to the person who didn't have it; at the
time it happens, it usually constitutes an exceedingly disagreeable
experience."*

—VILHJALMUR STEFANSSON, *MY LIFE WITH THE ESKIMO*

"Dear Mr. Pavlak, the Minnesota Bar Examiners regret to
inform you that you were unsuccessful on the July 2006 Minnesota Bar Examination…" The words on the page continued,
but my mind stopped. Life stopped. I attempted to process what
I had just read and what was happening, but my eyes kept reading and rereading the word *"unsuccessful." Oh my God!* I thought.
Not me…this cannot be happening to me. I stopped breathing
and went numb as my mind raced with terrible thoughts. The
chilly dusk that was descending on St. Paul, Minnesota, that
October evening seemed to be extinguishing my own vision of
the future as tears welled up in my eyes. The idyllic vision I had

of myself as an attorney was replaced with the apprehension of those dreadful questions I had done my best not to entertain for the last year.

My imagination ran wild. It unleashed a host of painful scenarios: the humiliating conversations with friends and family; the pain of having to begin—all over again—that soul-crushing regimen of studying for the exam, along with the collateral anxiety of waiting for my results; and, worst of all, the reality of being stuck indefinitely in this shitty not-a-student-but-not-a-lawyer status—no money, barely employed, and no means to pay off debt which now eclipsed $150,000.00. My mind balked and retreated into a surreal state of detachment. I was emotionally anesthetized, yet hyperaware. Dreadful scenarios unfolded in rapid succession about the next several months, possibly years: the humiliation of being known as a failure, being stuck in professional limbo, and perhaps never passing. I realized that the worst thing that could happen to me was about to happen to me. Having not taken a breath for almost a minute, I suddenly gasped. I could not contain the wellspring of emotion as tears dripped onto the letter in my hand. I did not move for almost twenty minutes. I was still standing alone under the glow of a single kitchen light in an otherwise dark house, reading over and over again that jarring sentence. Opening that letter had opened the door to a world of chaos, and life had just shoved me unwillingly across its threshold.

When I realized how long I had been standing motionless, I put the letter down, my mind racing. Suddenly, unable to focus or even sit still, I had to do something. I had to act. In a teary-eyed—almost zombie-like—state, I changed my clothes, got in my car, and drove to the Mississippi River about four miles away. I was so angered and overcome with so many different and indescribable emotions and feelings of inadequacy that I decided I would kick the shit out of myself and go for a run harder and faster than I ever had before. It was the only immediate way I would be able to expel the most amount of stress at one time. It was the one thing I could do to somehow mitigate the worrisome thoughts that were slowly consuming me.

The only illumination was provided by the golden street lamps of the parkway. I started my run on the St. Paul side of the river, ran southbound to the Ford Bridge and crossed it. Now on the Minneapolis side, I turned right onto the River Road Parkway and proceeded north. I passed all those charming homes I had seen as a child growing up—the ones I imagined doctors or lawyers lived in. On this night, as I ran past these homes noticing the warm glow of lights in a kitchen or dining room and seeing the silhouettes of their occupants, I imagined those same people enjoying dinner and uncorking wine as they discussed the day's work at the firm. I had wanted so badly to be on that trajectory and had envisioned myself one day, seven or eight years in the future, being a partner in a law firm and enjoying dinner in my own house. Instead on this night, I was trying to outrun those ugly and terrible feelings that were in hot pursuit. I finished the 5.3-mile run in under thirty-seven minutes—faster than I had ever run that route before. I drove home, again in silence. When I checked my phone, I saw that a few friends had passed congratulations via a group text which included me. I told no one. I took a shower. I went to bed.

As the weeks passed I began to wrestle with menacing thoughts of inadequacy. What began to afflict me the most was shame—whose true power comes from being unspeakable. Like everyone else, I had shared the expected date of my exam results with so many others that within a few days, people eventually asked me. It took everything for me to tell my parents that weekend when we were at my sister's house for dinner. My mom never went to college, and my dad completed his education piecemeal with night school. Through a steadfast work ethic, discipline, and incredible faith, they raised nine children on blue-collar wages to be God-fearing, productive citizens. They taught me the true meaning of hard work, sacrifice, and selflessness. I had wanted so badly to make them proud. If anyone knew how hard I had worked during these last three years, they did. Whenever I went to my parents' house for a decent meal, it was my mom who always tried to cheer me up and help lighten the burden she saw I was carrying. She was always doing her best to understand what school was like, and any gaps in her knowledge were filled with her maternal optimism that she had a son who was in law school. As I hung my head in shame and somberly told her I did not pass, she did the best she could to hold back her own tears and gave me a hug, wishing she could take away the pain she knew I carried. I felt completely alone, and she knew it.

In my arrogance and naïveté I had neglected to guard myself against the malign emotions of envy, avarice, selfishness, and insecurity. My devastation after failing the exam was commensurate with how a person transformed by law school into a hyper-competitive, hyper-vigilant, and status-driven individual would naturally react. Three years of being judged against the performance and abilities of others and living in a world where self-worth is largely determined by grade point average breeds envy and generally produces individuals who are both emotionally and spiritually ill-equipped to deal with setbacks. I felt completely impotent against this worst case scenario. Feelings of anxiety became more aggressive, and I became impatient with nearly everyone—especially fellow law school grads—which was really the manifestation of shame and embarrassment.

There is an unwritten, unspoken, and ethereal line separating those who are attorneys and those who are not. My attempt at self-preservation meant I withdrew from any modicum of a social life, especially from those with whom I just graduated and who had passed. I severed any tenuous relationships with people whose friendships in law school had formed as a matter of course. Besides a few close friendships I maintained, I realized I no longer had much in common with most of my fellow graduates.

Now that we were outside the academic walls, considering and beginning our own respective careers and futures, reasons to remain friends soon evaporated. Any common ground, in my mind, was extinguished when they became attorneys and I did not. Attempting to remain friends with them only sharpened my acrimonious feelings of inadequacy. I withdrew, and abruptly severing relationships was a byproduct of the emotional and spiritual vacuum that is the law school experience, which accentuates all the wrong ideals and cultivates social comparison bias.

Worse still, I began to doubt my own abilities. If I had slavishly studied for the previous three months—let alone three years—and it all resulted in failure, I faced the nagging question of how I might summon the confidence to know I would be able to accomplish even moderate goals I set for myself. Most troubling was that I had had a vision of my ideal self and it was not being met. This set me onto a path that led to my asking entirely different questions than my friends who were securing employment for themselves at law firms or as clerks for state and federal judges. They were contemplating questions like: *What high-rise condo should I live in? What car should I buy?* or even *Will you marry me?* Instead, I faced questions like: *How long could the rest of my life remain on hold? How much longer would I be straddling the gap between the worlds of student and lawyer? How long would I be able to sustain myself, especially when student loans come due? What if I do not pass the next time?*

These questions, and others like them, were dangerously close to the questions of survival. I realized I would have to make a living whether or not I was prepared to live on the fringes. Suddenly there was a sense of gravity to the normal expenses of everyday life. In other words, everything crystallized and became relevant because I could no longer assume I would be gainfully employed as an attorney and able to meet my obligations. Real trepidation set in as I had to face the possibility that I might spend the next several months—maybe years—in this odd status. Complicating things further was the fact that the Bar exam is only offered twice a year and blocking off four months at a time to study is difficult even in the best of circumstances.

The only solution, it seemed, was to try harder and study more fervently than ever. But as I considered that proposition, I thought, *My God, how? How in the world can I possibly give more of myself, my energy, and my focus to studying a second time than I did the first? Did I not work hard enough?* My mental tenacity had lost its grip. I was exhausted from being singularly fixated on my goal for the last three years. I had rarely taken breaks or given myself downtime from studying. My mental reserves of concentration and stamina were in short supply, and now over the last several months of preparation for the Bar exam, I had been profligate with those reserves. I had nothing left. Then there was the realization that I may have missed the best opportunity to pass the exam—when I had all the mental vigor, confidence, time, and motivation without the specter of recidivism hovering over every subsequent attempt. The most menacing thoughts were the prospects of not passing a second time, a third, or a fourth—perhaps never passing.[1]

If you are one of the unfortunate people who fails the Bar exam, your soul—reeling with the incessant social, academic, and professional comparisons made during law school—will have immense difficulty sustaining the embarrassment, shame, self-loathing, and hopelessness of that failure. On the surface, it means one will not be practicing law as planned. For many, this does not compute and leaves one bewildered as to how this could have happened. But there is something worse than bewilderment. It is something bitter; it is harsh and provokes immense anxiety as one peers into the abyss of chaos. If you are not prepared for it—and no one really ever is—it can be hell on earth.

After I failed the exam the first time, the future opened in front of me like a bottomless pit. I had what some psychologists call a numinous experience. And I never really awoke from my one-dimensional and trance-like state before taking the Bar exam a

---

1 Unfortunately, unlike many other tests in different disciplines, where performance gets better when you take the test over, this is not true of the Bar exam. Perhaps due to a psychological issue rather than an intellectual one, individuals who fail the Bar exam on their first attempt have very high failure rates on subsequent attempts.

second time in February 2007. When I failed that attempt, the consequential emotions of failure took on wild, almost demonic forms and plunged me into real trepidation. When everything was ripped out from underneath me, I identified with what all the externalities were telling me—*I was a failure.* This was a logical consequence of seeking external validation to the degree with which I had sought it. Hopelessness settled in, and my confidence withered away. My validation dissipated down to almost nothing. Unsurprisingly, the only active role I took in the aftermath of my failure was self-pity. I resorted to different and varying degrees of reclusiveness, isolation, and self-loathing. And I allowed these emotions to live rent-free in my soul for the next several years.

It is an all too real consequence for some who fail the Bar exam to find that the despair and hopelessness is so great it brings them to suicide; I have dedicated this book to one of them.[2]

Although I did not go that far, when I signed my name on the dotted line with the United States Marine Corps, I did consider how I would very likely be deployed to Iraq or Afghanistan. My emotional state being what it was, I was completely indifferent to the possibility of being killed in combat. And the reasons for my emotional detritus were nothing new. These feelings had begun their slow stranglehold of me approximately three years earlier when I first began law school.

---

2   Staci Zaretsky, "Recent Law School Graduate Commits Suicide after Failing Bar Exam," Above the Law, November 29, 2016, https://abovethelaw.com/2016/11/recent-law-school-graduate-commits-suicide-after-failing-bar-exam/.

Chapter 2

SCHADENFREUDE

"To feel envy is human, to savour schadenfreude is devilish."

—Arthur Schopenhauer, German philosopher

Envy is the great leveler of people's spirits, and if it cannot level things up, it will level them down. It begins by asking, *Why can't I have what others enjoy?*—and by the end of three years of law school, as classmates secure employment at prestigious law firms and judicial clerkships, envy demands, *Why should others enjoy what I may not?* At its best, envy is a motivator, a climber, and perhaps even a snob; at its worst, it is a destroyer. Rather than tolerate anyone happier than itself, it prefers to see everyone miserable together.

The literal meaning of the German word *schadenfreude* is "harm joy." There is no direct translation into English, but the root of this emotion is envy, which hates to see others happy. If you began law school unaware of the word's existence, at the end of your three years, you certainly and palpably felt it. More colloquially, *schadenfreude* is that quiet, internal pleasure we take when the misfortunes of others result in a benefit to ourselves.

Recently, the term has come to be known as "negative competition." Likewise, in the extremely competitive environment of law school, any academic mistake or shortcoming by one of your peers means that their status worsens while yours improves.

In law school, academic performance blurs the line between *doing one's best* and *being the best* because, for the vast majority of law students, they are one and the same. There are those with excellent grades at the top of the class and those with the not-so-excellent grades at the bottom. Whatever group one finds himself in, law school sows the seed of self-doubt and comparison to others. Each student contemplates his own potential in such a way that prohibits a capacity for healthy independent self-evaluation and internal validation. Law students tend to be highly institutionalized individuals who have thrived in competitive environments and view education as transactional: *I do excellent work and you give me high grades.* This only exacerbates the problem of seeking external validation. Many become fixated on what the institution and, by extension, the legal industry at large is demanding of them. Many law students and lawyers will always rise to the academic or professional challenge put in front of them, but often at the expense of their own fulfillment and internal validation.

Schadenfreude usually begins to set in—most poignantly for those in the lower half of the class—after first semester grades are published. It is then that the first-year (1L) student is struck with the cold reality that doing one's best no longer means being the best. No matter how talented, the insecurities and hyper-vigilance of one's status take center stage, making him poignantly aware of where he ranks in relation to his peers.

I had wanted to go to law school for several reasons, but in retrospect, few of them were good reasons. I went primarily as a means of attempting to change a paradigm, or rather to escape it. That paradigm as far as my incomplete understanding of it was concerned, was laden with never enough money, financial stress, and the exhaustion of raising a family. I grew up in a lower-middle class working family, the second oldest of nine children. Neither one of my parents was a traditional professional (e.g., teacher, engineer, lawyer, or doctor). They selflessly endured a hardscrabble life of hourly-wage employment to make ends meet and give their children opportunities. There were times I remember when they both worked two jobs; and in a family that size, every two years (sometimes less) a new baby would arrive robbing both of them of what little sleep they were already getting.

Adding to the fiscal demands of an eleven-person household, my parents, who valued private Catholic education, decided to send us to a parochial school in Minneapolis and later in St. Paul. But since they were never able to afford full tuition for each of their children, agreements were made with the school's administration that my siblings and I would participate in work-study programs to defray the costs. Likewise, we were expected to remain out of trouble and earn high grades. The former task was relatively easy due to my parents' discipline. Knowing the consequences of bad behavior, all nine of us children were considered very well-behaved kids who stayed out of trouble. The latter was something I had to work at. Since my older sister and I—beginning at ages twelve and ten, respectively—were responsible for babysitting even younger children and an infant, we were considered some of the most responsible and hardworking students in elementary and middle school.

But as I grew up, and especially as my older sister and I became the default babysitters when both parents were at work, I began to realize the costs of raising a family. In high school, my first job was as a busboy and dishwasher at a local restaurant, and I cherished every penny I received. I gained an immediate appreciation for how hard my parents worked and had been working their entire lives. My parents' financial stress was real, but I never knew the true particulars of their situation. We rarely ate at restaurants. We rarely even ate fast food. If we did go out to eat, it happened once every few years, often accompanying an extended family get-together with grandparents and cousins. We traveled little, and through what must have been Herculean efforts, my mom and dad did the best they could to occasionally take us on family vacations during the summer to lake resorts in northern Minnesota. My parents usually seemed to be only one crisis away from an empty checking account. Whether their savings account was in any better shape, I will never know.

What I did know was that my parents' normal state of being must have been exhaustion. Growing up and witnessing the stress of raising a family, indeed even helping to shoulder some of it as one of the eldest children, I made promises to myself that I would do it differently. Given the environment I grew up in, as I reflect on the choices I made, I am uncertain why I did not pursue a finance or business degree in undergraduate school. Instead, while taking philosophy as a freshman, I fell in love with the subject. I decided to major in it, despite the lack of an immediate and lucrative practical application.

After graduating from undergraduate school, I took a job as a part-time Latin teacher at a parochial school in a suburb of Minneapolis. (I had earned a minor in the language.) During those two years of teaching students how to decline nouns and adjectives, conjugate verbs, and improve their own English grammar and vocabulary, I thought about my next move. I even seriously considered whether I wanted to pursue a PhD in Philosophy. I went back to my three favorite philosophy professors from undergrad to ask them about how and why they pursued a doctorate and what their experience had been. Despite their enthusiasm for one of their own hoping to follow in their footsteps, they gave me a cold appraisal of the prospect of doing so.

One professor, whose class I immensely enjoyed, informed me of the nature of the job market, the shrinking philosophy departments throughout American universities, and the steep competition of landing a position, let alone securing tenure. "The job market," he said, "is pretty bad." Catching himself, he paused and then continued, "Actually, it's not just bad, it's awful. Pursuing a doctorate is one of the most challenging things you can do, professionally, and after all that work, the market for philosophy professors is paltry." After speaking to these gentlemen, I reconsidered pursuing philosophy. The prospect of living as a student for the rest of my twenties did not appeal to me. And I could not escape from the specter of how I was raised, where finances were thin and stress always present. A salary for a new philosophy professor, I thought, was insufficient for me to keep the promises I made to myself about doing things differently. I decided I would go to law school instead.

Becoming an attorney had crossed my mind in undergraduate school as I spoke to other philosophy students about what their plans were after graduation and how they were going to use this "useless" degree. Some of them said they were planning to attend law school, but most had no clue. No one in my family had ever been to law school. As far as I knew, no one had ever been to graduate school. One of the more significant errors I made was failing to investigate the day-in-the-life of an attorney and just what exactly the demands of law school would require. What propelled me was my desire to escape from a middle-class life, the stress, the worry, and hardships—known and unknown—of what my life might be if I could not command a high salary. What was high enough? I put no limits on it.

This was an attitude that would persist throughout my entire three years of law school, and have serious negative effects on me afterward. My limitless imagination continued to move the goal line for what I would consider a sufficient salary as an attorney. I continually added another $25K, $50K, or even $100K to the "ideal" amount I told myself would suffice. The problem with pursuing a law degree with these motives—as a vehicle to make my escape—is that I did not realize that by going to law school I was entering a certain paradigm. I entered a world of hyper-performing students, surgically focused on performance, class rank, aptitude, and the promise of securing a job as a practicing attorney. It was a world rife with cold competition, where only the top 10 percent of students are truly competitive in the job market, a microcosm of the academic "have and have-nots." Another oversight on my part was not understanding many attorneys do not make the kinds of salaries I thought I was destined for. And then, those who do, are beholden to the billable hour dissected into six-minute increments. Thus began my dangerously naïve attitude and narrative of success I told myself as I took the LSAT, got accepted, and encumbered myself with tens of thousands of dollars of student loans to secure my getaway car that would take me to the life I thought I wanted.

Each law school class comprises academically insecure, grade-obsessed, status-driven, overachievers competing against one another for grades, class rank, and ultimately jobs they seek as practicing attorneys. The biggest challenges to success are not necessarily the workload—though the amount of daily reading for a law student far exceeds anything he has ever done in undergrad. The greatest challenges come from the students' incessant comparison of themselves against the rest of their classmates. Law school is like "collecting a group of alcoholics and then opening the bar for three years."[3]

Each student is as equally bright and motivated as the next and nearly all have performed well in every previous undertaking, both inside and outside of the classroom. They have out-worked, out-shone, and out-done nearly all others for most of their lives with a fastidious work ethic and myopic vision of being the best. And while they may have paid lip service to the mantra *it's not about the grades, but about how much you learn,* internally, many do not care unless it is reflected in an "A" for their final grade. They are some of the most stubborn *alpha-students* of the academic world. Worse yet, the entire apparatus of law school places each student in competition with one another for the best grades in the class. This means a chance at getting into the best firms. The "best" firms are those that pay the highest salaries.

Law students tend to be above average in skepticism, competitiveness, urgency, autonomy, and how much they fixate on achievement. Skepticism showcases a tendency to be argumentative. Though this is hardly the benchmark one should use

---

3   This was a comment made by my Evidence professor Patrick Schiltz, who is now a federal district judge. See entire video at https://www.youtube.com/watch?v=BufcBAlyUo4.

when considering a career as an attorney. In fact, skepticism can impede inspiration, vision, and training in what might traditionally be called "soft skills." Urgency brings with it a need to "get things done" along with impatience, intolerance, and inadequate listening ability. Competitiveness, autonomy, and relentlessly pursuing achievement oftentimes create the byproducts of self-absorption, control, belligerence, and a personality that is extremely difficult to manage. Lawyers will often rank lower than the general population in sociability, interpersonal sensitivity, and resilience. They tend toward skepticism and emphasize analytic skill rather than interpersonal skills.[4] Unsurprisingly then, lawyers are notoriously the unhappiest group of professionals in America.[5]

There is also the tendency for law students and lawyers to have high needs for approval, regularly seeking the external validation of their peers and superiors. "The intention to look good often displaces the intention to be good."[6] Hand-in-hand with these perspectives is the additional notion that law students deem leadership education—what they view to be a spillover from MBA courses—as not intellectually sophisticated enough for the legal profession.

In general, overachievers, especially those who excel at analysis, do not normally possess a surplus of emotional intelligence,

---

4   Larry Richard, "Herding Cats: The Lawyer Personality Revealed," Report to Legal Management 29, no. 11 (August 2002): 4, 9 https://www.managingpartnerforum.org/tasks/sites/mpf/assets/image/MPF%20-%20WEBSITE%20-%20ARTICLE%20-%20Herding%20Cats%20-%20Richards1.pdf.

5   Anne M. Brafford, "Remodeling the 'Unhappiest Job in America,'" *Orange County Lawyer Magazine*, January 2014, 12, https://aspire.legal/app/uploads/2021/08/Reprint-OC-Lawyer-Jan-2014-Brafford-hi-res.pdf.

6   Robert Hargrove, *Masterful Coaching*, 3rd ed. (San Francisco: Jossey-Bass, 2008), 123.

making it difficult for them to relate to others or even empathize with them. Lawyers can also often be intimidating because of their command of voluminous amounts of information, which is useful in some legal settings (i.e., a courtroom or deposition), but it oftentimes serves them poorly because it can stifle collaboration, innovation, and easy engagement with others.

Moreover, the mental health among attorneys across America continues to be under severe strain. And the legal profession notoriously has one of the lowest job satisfaction rates in the world. A June 2022 report from the *ALM Intelligence 2022 Mental Health and Substance Abuse Survey* administered to over 3,400 respondents working at law firms of all sizes reported that the situation regarding the mental health of attorneys remains grave. The survey reports:[7]

> Thirty-five percent of respondents said they personally feel depressed, and two-thirds reported having anxiety. Three-quarters reported that the profession has had a negative effect on their mental health over time. Sixty-four percent reported that their personal relationships have suffered as a result of being a member of the legal profession. Nineteen percent answered yes to the question: "In your professional legal career, have you contemplated suicide?"

The law tends to attract those who have an indefatigable ambition for hyper-achievement which frequently leads to excessive focus on their performance and the impulse to surpass their competitors—striving higher and higher in search of lofty per-

---

7   Kristina Marlow, "Lawyers' Mental Health Remains in Crisis, but Awareness Is Growing," Above the Law, June 17, 2022, https://abovethelaw.com/2022/06/lawyers-mental-health-remains-in-crisis-but-awareness-is-growing/.

sonal achievement. "These tendencies and narcissism too often go uncorrected in legal workplaces…[and] over time, these dynamics can further reinforce perceptions of entitlement and compromise the capacity to learn from mistakes."[8] Worse still, the methodical, procedural, and logical way lawyers like to work (and what society appreciates about them) is more or less incongruent with dynamic and changing environments. Lawyers will patiently (or impatiently) wait for all the details they need to be equipped to answer all questions they might get from the bench and be a zealous advocate. They want to have all the facts because an entire line of questioning, brief, or trial could turn on the knowledge or ignorance of one piece of information. Lawyers therefore tend to be risk averse when their own decisions are on the line, and they would preferably wait for as much information as possible before offering advice or choosing a particular path.

In addition to the insecurities of one's peer group in law school, another problem facing law students and newly minted attorneys is a saturated legal industry. Instead of limiting the quota on the number of law students as the medical field does for future doctors, the solution was to simply open more law schools. The second consequence of an unlimited quota is the perpetuation of the naïve idea of the income potential for attorneys. Many refuse to believe they are destined to make $60K a year. There are plenty of stories of unemployed or under-employed attorneys forced to supplement their income as Uber drivers, bartenders, and even pivot into other industries and only

---

8   Deborah L. Rhode, "What Lawyers Lack: Leadership," *University of St. Thomas Law Journal* 9, no 2 (Winter 2011): 477, https://ir.stthomas.edu/cgi/viewcontent.cgi?referer=&httpsredir=1&article=1274&context=ustlj.

occasionally perform work as an attorney due to a saturated legal market.[9]

Ultimately, the expectation mismanagement of both undergraduate and law schools, irresponsible lending by banks, and inadequate accountability about who is filling their rosters, encumbers many attorneys with crushing debt and bleak professional outlooks. Since the mid-1990's law school enrollments have ballooned to outpace the number of available legal jobs by almost two to one. I frankly should have never been admitted to law school in the first place. My LSAT score was unremarkable and too low to make me competitive for placement at a top-tier law school; my undergraduate grades, decent and above average, were not earth-shattering. Nor did I have any on-the-job training as a paralegal or even a clerk.

Ruthless comparison and the desire for external validation sets in because, unlike any other academic environment, for the first time, there is an institutional mechanism in place preventing all of us from receiving the grades we would become so accustomed to for most of our lives—*the curve*. In other words, we could not all get "A's" anymore.

The curve is not specific to law school, but its application is

---

9   An excellent book on the costs of becoming an attorney is *The Lawyer Bubble: A Profession in Crisis* by Steven J. Harper (New York: Basic Books, 2013). The book discusses some of the misguided expectations of young college graduates who shell out tens of thousands of dollars on a legal education in search of a degree they hope will lead to a more promising and lucrative career. According to Harper, in 2013, the average debt of a graduate from an ABA-accredited law school was almost one hundred thousand dollars [which is in addition to any debt incurred from undergraduate studies] (Harper, *Lawyer Bubble*, 4), but the median income for all lawyers who graduated in 2011 was approximately sixty thousand dollars (Harper, *Lawyer Bubble*, 6). For the vast majority of graduates, earning a law degree will never yield a return equal to the financial cost of becoming a lawyer.

not created equal. (Disclaimer: to any engineers who may be reading this, I pass no judgment about the ease, difficulty, or complexity of classes essential to that profession.) The difference is, for example, in engineering classes, due to the incredible difficulty of the problems and subject matter—the *test* is curved, so that even at the extreme unlikelihood of it occurring, all students in, for instance, a Fluid Dynamics class, at least have a chance of earning an "A." The curve is manifest in the exam itself, so that as applied to the test, an original overall score of 35 percent is now the "A" and the professor awards the rest of the grades from there.

There are roughly 120–130 law students in a first-year law school class. The first year curriculum at nearly every law school in the country is the same: first semester has Contracts, Torts, Constitutional Law, and Legal Writing I; second semester has Civil Procedure, Property, Criminal Law, and Legal Writing II. So whether you are attending an Ivy League school or a small state school in the Midwest the first year is the same and even includes many of the same textbooks and much of the same case law. Put another way, with the myriad of study guides, full disclosure of syllabi with reading assignments, and what is expected of the student and what he can expect on the final exam, the student has all the answers at his disposal in one form or another. In law school, the curve is applied to the *students*.

Generally, there are no quizzes, tests, or regular homework assignments to be turned in for grading during the semester. Some law schools may offer a relatively inconsequential midterm exam in order to help students appraise where their own understanding lies, but they tend to be worth almost no point value and a vast majority of law schools do not do this.

Instead the singular responsibility of the law student is to read and understand every issue presented throughout the semester—all in preparation for a cumulative final exam.

In general, lawyers do not have the time to pursue the lofty goals of jurisprudential thought and dissecting a problem from all philosophical aspects. The answers to those questions (as fulfilling as they may be to the human spirit) and finding purpose frankly do not put food on the table. We had to learn how to take the law for what it was and learn how to apply it to the real-life facts. I had to learn how to work within it. The focus of the curriculum is predominantly on analytic reasoning, substantive knowledge, research, and writing. The upshot is the law student cannot help but be influenced by the issue recognition and razor sharp logic of legal writing and thinking, by completely immersing himself into the world of case law. Through the slow, page-after-page percolation of reading legal opinions throughout the three years of law school, the student learns how to think and communicate like an attorney.

In some sense, the entire legal industry is not necessarily in pursuit of the truth. It seemed to pay lip service to ideas like "justice" and "fairness" and "equality," but longer, more in-depth philosophical discussions about what those ideas meant were pushed aside. Instead, it was a place where we would learn to play rhetorical games, using our persuasive powers on behalf of any cause—however unworthy or perverse the logic—all in return for payment. It seemed we were being groomed to be rhetorical strategists, perhaps amoral, and disinterested in truth, suggesting that all that really mattered was winning. We slowly replaced the objective notion of "justice" with what might be the subjective desires of the client and zealously advocated for those desires. In other words, we seemed to equivocate justice and fairness with the prerogatives of an individual for whom we might advocate. We would be hired hands, traveling wordsmiths who sold their skills to the highest bidder. As I read my case law, I realized that the best lawyers displayed a remarkable capacity for finessing the nuances of language. Any demands of conscience or collective responsibility, shared values, and respect for tradition were all put at risk by the relentless promotion of self-interest.

I quickly realized the law is really more about selling your skills as a problem-solver of day-to-day issues that arise and prohibit others from moving forward with their own lives, than it is about the lofty pursuit of justice on some esoteric level. I was learning a trade; and just like a plumber, electrician, or carpenter learns how to use their tools to solve problems, lawyers apply a different set of tools to solve legal ones.

At the end of my first year, I was unhappy with my state in life and was extremely insecure about my own academic and professional abilities. Still, I had to come to terms with the grades I had received and a stark reality hit me. First, this will be a much more difficult endeavor than I had originally planned and second, despite my hardest work and best efforts there are people who were simply better at this than I. This last point was particularly difficult to accept. The hard work I was doing day in and day out, week in and week out, month after month, still did not always matter because I was earning average grades. Law school has a certain way of humbling you in an area most have always excelled.

The law student has to learn how to take things in stride and where your abilities are, respective to others. But because the nature of law school and the hiring process is based on those comparisons to others, and your grades are the metric by which you are measured against everyone else, it cannot help but create a very cold and contentious environment.

If you are lucky enough to participate in on-campus interviews and even luckier to secure a summer associate position at one of the large firms, you will work between your second and third year of law school. Considering the meager standard of living over the last eighteen months, your hourly rates for that summer will be a welcome respite from what has, up to that point, been a rather austere lifestyle. During the late fall or early winter of third year, the summer associates who made a good impression and, most importantly, were well-liked by the partners they worked for can expect to receive job offers for positions beginning after graduation and the Bar exam.

Thus there is a simple crescendo into a six-figure salary. It begins with your first semester grades, then second semester grades, then on-campus interviews, then summer associate, and finally the offer to become an attorney at the same firm in under a year's time. Hence, in a little over two years, one can go from being a "twenty-something" second-year law student living on ramen noodles to being a practicing attorney making a salary of $150K/annum (now $215k/annum at some firms).[10] And although some make it look effortless, it is no easy task. The problem is that there is no other mechanism for the rest of the 90 percent to get to a top-tier law firm directly out of law school. It is every

10   Meghan Tribe, "Cravath Tops Rival Davis Polk's Associate Pay Scale, up to $415k," Bloomberg Law, February 28, 2022, https://news.bloomberglaw.com/business-and-practice/cravath-tops-rival-davis-polks-associate-pay-scale-up-to-415k.

person for themselves. What is interesting is that a year or eighteen months earlier, upon entering law school and meeting your classmates on orientation day, you may have been determined to only be a prosecutor, a public defender, or a transactional attorney dealing in contracts. But after the dust of first year has settled, and the stark reality of your grades has sunk in, you realize you may have no options or bargaining power at all. You will have to take whatever you can get—and it may be nothing.

The day after I graduated from law school, I was lucky enough to take a week's vacation at a resort in Acapulco, Mexico, courtesy of a classmate who had become a good friend. My friend's wife and two other classmates joined us. We graduated around 3:00 p.m. on Saturday, May 13, 2006. By 6:00 a.m. the next morning, our plane's main cabin door had been closed and we pulled away from the gate. The five of us were exhausted from a night of drinking and celebrating, but gleeful about spending the next six days at an incredible resort. The stress of the most challenging academic experience we had ever faced was finally behind us, and it melted away like the ice in our cocktails under the intense sun and tropical heat of southern Mexico. The days were long and lazy, punctuated with tequila shots, well-deserved catnaps, and throwing a Frisbee on the beach as the Pacific Ocean, warm as bath water, lapped at our ankles. It was exactly what we needed. The reverie was merely the calm before the storm. We had survived everything law school could throw at us. But even on the beach amid the laughter, relaxation, and high-fives, the Bar exam, which previously had been looming on the horizon, was rapidly approaching and would be bearing down on us when we returned to Minnesota. The next two and a half months would be filled with the mounting pressure and anxiety of preparing for the most important exam of my life.

Chapter 3

THE BAR EXAM

"But there is a story—and I believe it is true—a guy has a heart attack during the bar exam and is on the floor. Someone taking the test, who happens to be a doctor, tends to him. But then the proctors won't give any extra time to complete the exam."
—CYNTHIA L. COOPER, STUDENT LAWYER, 31 NO. 6, 2003

Day One. For the two days of the Bar exam, the last Tuesday and Wednesday of July, the entire body of new graduates from the four law schools across the Twin Cities descended upon River Center in St. Paul, Minnesota. The same thing would be happening in every state around the country. Leaving absolutely nothing to chance, I arrived at the venue approximately ninety minutes early bringing all the correct documentation with me—most importantly my examinee number that the Minnesota State Bar Association had mailed to me a few weeks earlier. *Woe to the examinee who forgot this essential piece of paper the morning of the exam.* That, along with two forms of identification guaranteed my entrance into the exam. I also carried a small clear Ziplock bag containing the only materials that were allowed in the examination room: No. 2 pencils, erasers, earplugs, and an analog watch.

I checked in with my examination number and two forms of identification. I was given a lanyard that would display the document I had just used to enter. I would find the same number on a table inside the exam room. I saw a few people whom I knew. I walked over to meet them. We greeted each other with an air of anxious restiveness. We could read the tension in each other's eyes: *Let's just get this over with.* We had about ten minutes to kill with idle chatter—no one dared jinx it by asking a question of real legal substance, so we talked about the night before, what we had for dinner, when we finally went to bed, and our morning routine.

We were split into two groups: those taking the exam on a computer and those hand-writing it. I was in the latter group along with many others—all of us too scared to put our trust in a machine for the biggest test of our lives. People shuddered at the thought of the unlikely, though nevertheless possible catastrophe of one's screen going black, a power surge, or any instance of Murphy's Law. (The middle of an essay on Real Property is not the opportunity to practice and refine one's IT troubleshooting skills.) What is more, there was always the possibility of losing your answers because of the test's software simply malfunctioning, thus losing everything you had typed.

Still, the second group taking the exam on their computers assessed the risk and determined the chance that an "exam ending" event was remote. So they opted for the more pragmatic approach. The upshot of taking the exam on the computer, notwithstanding the attendant risks, are threefold:

1. Typeface is more legible than handwriting. The mantra of the essay graders being, *If I can't read it, then you didn't write it.*
2. Formatting issues can be dealt with much more quickly and efficiently.
3. If and when the examinee knows time is running out, he could simply type the keywords of the legal issue and hopefully even a rule of law and quickly bulletize his analysis—at least getting something down on paper. Without question, this can be done more quickly and likewise more legibly than hand-writing. And where there is an issue or rule, there are points to be had. The bottom line being, if you are in a time crunch, you will wish you were using a computer.

At 8:40 a.m. the lead proctor walked up to the podium and with a maternal, but firm voice said, "Good morning. Welcome to the July 2006 Minnesota State Bar Examination." She began the instructions on how to complete the several pages of paperwork that would really be the only proof that we actually took the damn thing. It was the paperwork that married the examinee to the exam. It was 8:50. Next, she explained that the proctors were available to answer any minor questions during the exam, but more importantly, the proctors were a security measure against cheating. Nothing could be retrieved from our belongings after the exam had begun. They were also required to accompany us *into* the restroom. Finally, they patrolled the ballroom to ensure there was absolutely no talking among examinees. We risked immediate dismissal, and our tests being discarded, upon any suspicion of cheating.

For the next three hours, I would be answering six essay questions taken from fourteen areas of Minnesota law. The morning session would end promptly at noon. We would have an hour lunch break. Back in our seats by 1:15 p.m.; the afternoon session would begin at 1:30. The afternoon session was the Multistate Performance Test and would last another three hours. The next day would also last six hours and consist entirely of multiple choice questions.

At 9:00 a.m., the test began. For each essay question, I would have approximately ten to twelve minutes to read the fact pattern and outline my answer—identifying every legal issue and sub-issue I could find. I would then have eighteen to twenty minutes to write my answer. Time management would be crucial. As each thirty-minute window comes to an end, the candidate must be able to make the important decision of whether to continue writing or move on to the next essay. *Do I remain on this answer for an extra four to five minutes in order to write what I know will be a better, more complete answer?* The catch is, doing so would mean being five minutes behind on the next essay, which could result in a cascade effect, from essay to essay, with the candidate never making up ground. Where time management is crucial for success, one of the best ways to manage it is to stop writing and move on.

Regardless of where you take the Bar exam, each jurisdiction grades the essays the same way. Each is given three reads by practicing attorneys who, after a regular day's work, come home and pore over hundreds of essays—getting paid by the state's Bar Association by the hour. This means that in order to make it worth their while, the more essays they read per hour the better for them. So, organization, legibility, and verbatim rules of law are all paramount to making it as easy as possible for the grader to grade your essay.

"Pencils down!"

Suddenly it was 12:00. All of us had been hastily scribbling our final words into our blue books (the bound books of blank paper in which we wrote our essays). Hundreds of pencils simultaneously dropped to the tables accompanied by one large collective gasp exhaling the last bit of stress bottled up inside that morning. No one dared keep writing after time had been called for fear of being seen by a vigilant proctor, suspected of cheating, and having his or her exam discarded. We broke for an hour lunch.

The afternoon session was the Multistate Performance Test (MPT). The candidate, acting as a practicing attorney, receives instructions from a fictitious managing partner or city prosecutor by way of an interoffice memo. The candidate must glean the task or tasks to perform, read a library of case law or controlling authorities, determine the legal issues in controversy, and write a memo, brief, letter to the client, or a motion…in three hours.

Day Two. The Multistate Bar Exam (MBE) is 200 multiple choice questions covering what is commonly referred to as the "big six."[11] It tests the black-letter law of what the American Bar Association considers the six basic, and most frequently occurring, areas that every attorney should know, and for which the law has generally remained the same. The MBE is a predictor of whether an applicant will pass the exam because it is more about eliminating the wrong answers than choosing the right one. The nuance being, if all of the answers are incorrect,

---

11 The six areas of law covered in the MBE were Contracts, Torts, Real Property, Criminal Law and Procedure, Evidence, and Constitutional Law. However, as of 2015, the American Bar Association now includes Civil Procedure on this portion of the exam.

the examinee's understanding of the law ought to be good enough to see the logic behind choosing the best response. The examinee does himself a disservice if he relies on sheer memory because then he will look for the answer his mind recognizes and has been training for, rather than being able to read between the lines and determine what each question is really asking.

The morning session unfolded without incident, except there was no time to check my answers—no time to reflect on what the examiners were really asking. I was on question #90 when I realized only eight minutes remained. I had to hurry. I flipped the last remaining pages of my test booklet forward looking for short fact patterns—Evidence or even Constitutional Law—and answered them as quickly as I could, trying to buy back valuable time.

The afternoon session began the same way every prior session had, except this time when we entered the room there was an air of less pressure, less anxiety—less stress. The room felt lighter. After I finished question 165 that afternoon, the weight, stress and exhaustion of the last three months slowly enveloped me. I felt as if I were in the last five minutes of running a marathon—except it was my mind that was exhausted. I looked up at the clock, I had twenty minutes left. I was on question 189—near perfect pace for the 1.8 minutes per question ratio.

"Pencils down."

A collective sigh could be heard across the ballroom accompanied by murmurings of relief and euphoric giggles. The results were now out of our hands. I gathered up my testing materials and utensils, stood up, and stretched. My mind was mush. I met my friends outside; we laughed (we could not help it) and shook hands. We walked across the street to a local bar. We had only one thing left to do: drink away the stress of the last four months. But it would be another three months before I learned my fate, which would turn my life upside down.

In the aftermath of my Bar exam failures, I realized I had spent three years of my life seeking external validation in nearly everything I did. I came to understand the problem with law school is that its mechanisms of evaluation, grading, and stratifying students creates in them a necessity of acceptance. My professors determined how well I had mastered certain material, but they judged me not against a static metric, but rather against the metric of other students in class. Not only had the last three years made me a perfectionist and an academic narcissist, but the very things I came to identify with—grades, GPA, and class rank—were validated (or invalidated) by the performance of my peers. Unfortunately, I had never paused long enough to determine whether this perspective on the world truly added value to my life. I was surrounded by 120 others who were behaving mostly the same way I was. Every other law student was a mirror of my narcissism.

The more sinister lesson I learned was that I was entirely unprepared for failure. It had stopped all forward progress towards my goal, and it presented me with questions I had never entertained before. The comfortable, predictable, rewarding present had vanished. Failure was not supposed to be part of my reality, and now it had implications for everything. My long-term goals had to be reoriented and recalibrated after having been demolished. I had done everything in my power and control to eradicate the possibility of this very thing from occurring; now the emptiness of the unknown was staring me in the face. I was peering into uncharted territory, entirely unprepared for what I might encounter.

If all one does is define himself by GPA, class rank, status, financial promise, and being a part of the most prestigious firms, then it should be no surprise that any obstacle to achieving those things—up to and including failure—will have a devastating effect on what he thinks of himself. In my case, I defined myself by inadequacy, failure, and lacking potential. During law school, I had assigned my entire identity to transient, superficial, and insubstantial criteria. Any sense of equanimity had been eroded by three years of grinding and superficial academic pursuits.

PART II

CROSSING THE
THRESHOLD

Chapter 4

WHY THE MARINE CORPS?

"The United States Marine Corps, with its fiercely proud tradition of excellence in combat, its hallowed rituals, and its unbending code of honor, is part of the fabric of American myth. "
—THOMAS E. RICKS; *MAKING THE CORPS*, 1997

I was six years old. In the summer of 1985, my parents took a family vacation from Minnesota to Disney World. We stopped along the way to visit my uncle, who was a Navy Corpsman at the time and stationed at Camp Lejeune, North Carolina. We stayed for two days, and he wanted to get me something to remember the visit. So when we were at the Post Exchange on base, he bought me a tri-color eight-point garrison cover. (In the Marine Corps, headgear is not called a hat, it's called a cover.) The next day, as we were leaving base excited to be on our way to Florida, my dad was driving in the left-hand lane when a small convoy of Marine Humvees (High Mobility Multipurpose Wheeled Vehicles) began to pass in the right lane. As they approached, my dad said, "Chris, put your cover on and look out the window." I quickly scrambled to find it amid our luggage. I put it on and rested my chin on my crossed arms as I looked out the window. I watched, mesmerized, as the hulking, rumbling convoy drove past. Proudly wearing my cover, I felt connected to them if only because I was wearing the same kind of clothing they were. Then, as if to remove any doubt about my inclusion into their group, the Marine driving the Humvee looked down, saw me, and saluted me. I never forgot that. From then on, I was resolved—if I were ever to join the military, I would only join the Marine Corps.

During my second year of law school, I decided I wanted to become a federal prosecutor. This turned out to be a more difficult task than simply telling myself I would become one. It required pedigree, grades, class rank, and elusive legal experience to make it into a U.S. Attorney's office. Given my own class standing, lackluster performance, and inability to secure a clerkship or summer internship at a prosecutor's office, the deck was stacked against me.

As time went on, I developed a single-minded fixation on joining the Marines. I would spend late nights in the library looking at Marine Corps websites, blogs, posts, and Google images. I was determined to learn everything I could about an organization I so badly wanted to be a part of.

I learned of an alternative to whatever might be considered a "regular" path to the U.S. Attorney's office—become a Staff Judge Advocate (SJA). Military lawyers follow the Uniform Code of Military Justice and are practicing, for all intents and purposes, federal law. Many SJAs receive a license to practice in federal court as they matriculate through their respective branch's justice school. These schools are part of the service member's officer training after they have earned their commission. The Army, Navy, and Air Force each have their own justice school of varying lengths. Marines attend Naval Justice School with other Navy SJAs in Rhode Island.

While it would not guarantee a position as a federal prosecutor, becoming an SJA and obtaining four to eight years of experience practicing federal law in the military would likely give an applicant a competitive edge. Based on the promise I had made to myself as a child, I made up my mind to join the United States Marine Corps.

I met Ken Connelly in law school, and he became a friend and personal mentor. Although he was one academic year behind me, he was about seven or eight years older than I, with more interesting life experience than a typical law student. When I got to know him, he was already in his mid-thirties, married, with two children. I first met him one day in between classes. We had known each other for about two months since we belonged to the same extracurricular groups and loose circle of friends. During our first substantive conversation, I learned he was a former Logistics Officer in the Marine Corps.

Ken personifies everything one might imagine of an Irish Catholic New Yorker. His acerbic wit and sarcasm take proverbial "ball-breaking" to new heights. We all liked him immediately. But under the abrasive veneer was a man of both sharp intelligence and immense humility. Amidst the hyper-competitive and intellectually narcissistic attitudes of so many of my peers, Ken could have easily had the biggest ego of all, with the pedigree to back it up. He will not tell you he graduated with honors from Dartmouth in literature, that he earned his master's degree with honors from Fordham, or how, after his Marine Corps service, he was ranked in the top 10 percent of his law school class. Ken Connelly was above the fray.[12] He simply did not care what others thought of him in a place where everybody cared what others thought of themselves.

Another source of influence was a gentleman I met about eight months after I met Ken: Marine Lieutenant Colonel Bob Stephenson. As I began to explore ways I might be able to become a federal prosecutor via first becoming a military lawyer, I learned that Lt. Col. Stephenson (a Cobra pilot) had mobilized as a reservist to take a deployment to Iraq from 2004–2005 and, having recently returned, would be hosting a slideshow question-and-answer period about his deployment. This would be the first time I would meet a Marine and get the ground truth about what it was like and some possible insight into whether it would be worth it to pursue a career in the military as a lawyer.

During Operation Iraqi Freedom, several forward operating bases (FOBs) had either a regimental combat team (RCT) or a Marine Expeditionary Unit (MEU) based at them. In the case of FOB Kalsu, it was the 24th MEU. In July 2004, the 24th MEU, 1st Marine Division, assumed command of FOB Kalsu, using it as a command post for operations in Iraq's Anbar Province, the areas south of Baghdad, and then subsequently, the assault on Fallujah in November 2004. The 3rd Marine Air Wing (MAW) was in charge of the airspace for

---

12   Ken ended up graduating with honors in the top 10 percent of his law school class, securing a federal clerkship in Arizona before going to work for the largest law firm in Minneapolis. He then moved back to Arizona.

the entire country/theater. The MAW wanted a representative at each FOB. Likewise Lt. Col. Stephenson was responsible for all aviation detachments at FOB Kalsu—refuelers, ordinance, expeditionary airfield Marines, air traffic control tower, and COMM squadron detachments going into or out of FOB Kalsu. He indicated it was a billet created specifically for Operation Iraqi Freedom.

In less than a year, I had met two men whom I would ultimately look up to as mentors and role models, not only professionally, but personally. They had something I didn't, and I knew it. And I knew whatever it was, I was not getting it in law school—in fact, just the opposite. What I saw in them was a nonchalant attitude about what others thought about them. They were confident, but not arrogant. They were professional, but not stuffy. And best of all, they were accessible and did not think themselves better than anyone else. It took me a long time to articulate what it was they possessed, difficult to define and something I had not seen before—professional nonchalance—a commingling of restraint and detachment.

Lt. Col. Stephenson maintained a strong Marine Corps network in the Twin Cities metro area, and he introduced me to a former Marine SJA named Jim Haase. Two weeks after I met Lt. Col. Stephenson, I met Jim at his office in St. Paul, where he worked in the Attorney General's office. I sat down across a desk strewn with legal research, notepads, and legal treatises. Jim was an open book and was actually more excited to discuss Marine Corps experiences than his current day-to-day experiences as a lawyer in the AG's office. So eager, in fact, that he took out a photo album of his deployment to Iraq. As he got up from his chair and walked toward the bookshelf in his office, a brief pause in the conversation allowed me to ask him directly, "Why did you join the Marine Corps?"

He responded, "Because Marines are different."

He told me about the men whom he considered mentors and how they treated him. "No matter what might be happening, they always gave me their full attention," Jim said. He recalled that his mentors included him immediately in the conversation, the event, or the experience. Not only did Jim speak with incredible pride about his photo album (as he leaned way over his desk to point out the details to me) and the experiences it captured, but he actually gave it to me to page through, sharing a bit of himself with a total stranger. Then he finished his answer. "It's a state of mind," he said. "Everyone I met seemed to imply the Marine Corps is more than a job." And he added, "I learned that becoming a Marine is an identity."

I began to realize that the Marine Corps is a special group of people who are seeking to identify with an ideal, rather than simply join an organization. Jim continued showing me pictures, and the conversation eventually changed to his current job in the AG's office. He said, "It's a good job, but not nearly as dynamic or as fun as my deployments or being an SJA, but life goes on." He finally said what I had already been thinking—every single Marine he met before he joined could not see themselves in any other branch of service.

Jim said he thought it would be a good idea for me to meet a colleague of his, another attorney in the office who had come from a different branch of service (a former Army JAG). He indicated I *owed* it to myself to explore the *options* of each branch of service. Jim called his colleague, and he walked me down to the office. He was a younger man than Jim and had left the Army as a captain—Jim was still a major in the Reserves. I asked him the same kind of question I asked Jim: "Why did you join the Army?" I could already feel a different vibe. We sat across from one another, his desk between us. There were no photo albums, no noticeable memorabilia, and only a few stories. Then I realized that he was referring to his experiences as something he had done, as if it were a past life. He had been an attorney in the Army, a respectable occupation, but being a soldier did not seem to be how he identified himself. I was grateful for his time, and he said I could reach out if I had any other questions. After a rather short meeting, we shook hands, and I left. These were the differences I began to notice between the branches of service, but perhaps the ultimate distinction of the Marines came at the end of my meeting with Jim.

I returned to Jim's office, but before I left, he asked me if I would be interested in shadowing some Marine friends who were still on active duty in San Diego and Camp Pendleton that summer. I would be able to spend a week with Marine SJAs to get a snapshot of what it might be like to be an attorney in the Marines. I said yes immediately. This gesture of help and generosity, of going above and beyond what was expected, offering to help someone he hardly knew, simply because I was *interested* in the Marine Corps was the first of many gestures of pride, selflessness, and esprit de corps I realized were part of the Marine Corps ethos: to help a buddy go the extra mile and set him up for success.

For the rest of the semester and the entire summer of 2005, I learned everything I could about the Marine Corps. I looked at websites after I became too tired to study; I read blogs; I read interviews with Marines who were returning from Iraq and Afghanistan. I watched as many videos as I could find on the then-new website YouTube.com. I picked Ken Connelly's brain and continued to meet with Bob Stephenson, craving any information relating to the Marines. The first book I read on the subject was *Making the Corps* by Thomas Ricks.

I arrived in San Diego, at the Marine Corps Recruit Depot, the day the captain I would be shadowing was in the middle of moving offices from one end of the building to the other. He stopped what he was doing and gave me his undivided attention. I told him I could come back later, but he insisted that I was not a distraction and wanted to continue the conversation. So we found another vacant office and chatted for nearly an hour.

I explained how I had met Jim, what my intent for being there was, and what I would like to do that week if it were possible. He was an open book and completely candid about his experiences and the day-to-day of being an SJA. I joined him and the other Marines in his shop for physical training (PT); I sat in on his client meetings, went to oral arguments, and even visited a client of his who was currently in the brig at the Marine Corps base on Miramar. Throughout the week, he introduced me to his colleagues and superiors; all of them were enthusiastic that I was considering joining the Marine Corps.

I returned to Minnesota, just before the beginning of my third and final year of law school, with a new vigor. After being somewhat ambivalent about what specific area of the law interested me for the last two years, I finally had something I could call my own, and a vision of myself that I could execute, outside of the normal paper chase occurring among my classmates. I would become an SJA in the Marine Corps. I finally felt a sense of peace as I was able to articulate what it was I would do after graduation and passing the Bar exam. A huge weight had been lifted off my shoulders. After being in touch for several months with the local Officer Selection Officer (OSO), I returned to his office with the complete conviction that I wanted to be an SJA in the Marines.

Then came the bad news.

The Marine Corps forecasts how many lawyers will be leaving the active duty forces and how many more it will need each year. Likewise, Headquarters Marine Corps informs its OSOs about any depletion or potential depletion in the numbers of lawyers across the fleet and instructs them about how many more the Marine Corps can sustain and should recruit. It calculates how long each one's training evolution will be all the way from Officer Candidates School (OCS) to Naval Justice School (approximately nine months later) and up to where they will be stationed. My OSO informed me that the Marine Corps quota for attorneys was already full for his recruiting office.

In other words, the Marine Corps did not need more attorneys no matter where they came from or what their commissioning source was. That is, whether they attended OCS during one of their summer vacations from college or waited until after college graduation to attend OCS, the numbers were already met. One of the last responses Captain Gawronski received from a counterpart at Headquarters Marine Corps in Quantico, and which he forwarded in an email to me, included the phrases, "[w]e simply don't have that mission right now. Tell the guy he may want to consider a different branch."

A different branch?! I said to myself, as I read the email, incredulous at the possibility. By this time, I had become friends with several Marines, been the beneficiary of their help, gone to San Diego and shadowed them, been an invited guest of Bob Stephenson to the Marine Corps Ball, and been in touch with the OSO since March (it was now December 2005), and I would be taking the Bar exam in July 2006. After everything I had learned, people I had met, and perhaps going all the way back to that salute I received on the way to Disney World when I was five years old, there was no other branch for me. Now I was being told that I would not be able to become an attorney in the Marines, and there was nothing I could do about it.

I was so certain that I wanted to be an SJA that I had forfeited looking at regular civilian jobs, clerkships, and internships. I would be graduating in only five months, and I had nothing lined up. Those fears of not knowing what I would do and being jobless, which had been quelled with the certainty of wanting to be an SJA, now crept slowly back into my mind.

As I looked back on the last two and a half years of law school and at the insecure, selfish, and generally unhappy person I had become, I did not like what I saw. And now for nearly the last year, I had been exposed to a world of teamwork, camaraderie, esprit de corps, unselfishness, and service—a world that was the opposite of the *schadenfreude* that had come to be my baseline emotion in life. I would be turning twenty-seven in April. My age window for even being a Marine at all was rapidly closing too (I would need an age waiver at twenty-eight years old). The thought crossed my mind, *Should I join the Marines anyway?* I asked Ken Connelly what he thought about the idea. All he told me was, "It's never a bad decision to become an officer in the Marine Corps."

"Even if I'm not an attorney?" I pressed.

"Yes," he replied. "There'll be time later to practice law if you want, but if you miss this opportunity, you'll never get it back."

Just over a year later, still reeling from my first Bar exam failure, and in the middle of preparing for my second attempt scheduled for February 2007, I drove to Captain Gawronski's office and signed on the dotted line as a ground contract with the United States Marine Corps on January 26, 2007. In April, just after my twenty-eighth birthday, I learned I had failed the Bar exam a second time.

Chapter 5

THE ROAD OF TRIALS

*"The big question is whether you are going to say a hearty 'yes' to
your adventure."*

—Joseph Campbell

On June 2, 2007, I boarded a plane with several other officer
candidates from Minnesota and Iowa bound for Washington,
DC. We had been given instructions that, upon arriving at
Ronald Reagan Washington National Airport, we were to make
our way to the street level of the concourse to a baggage carou-
sel off the beaten path of normal airport traffic. There, we would
be picked up by Marines who would shuttle us to Quantico
approximately thirty-five miles south of DC in Virginia. All of
the officer candidates coming from all over the United States
had also been instructed to meet at the specific location of
the airport. We were easy to spot. All of us were wearing the
Marine Corps version of "proper civilian attire"—khaki trousers with a tucked-in polo shirt. I noticed the prior enlisted
Marines who already had their hair cut short as part of their
normal grooming standards. Soon enough my hair would be
just as short.

The Marines who met us were corporals and lance corporals only two or three ranks above the lowest ranking enlisted Marines. They were wearing their Service-C uniforms (khaki short-sleeved shirts with green trousers). Their uniforms looked impeccable. They yelled all kinds of directions: "GET OVER HERE! PUT YOUR GEAR DOWN! NOW PICK UP YOUR GEAR! GET ON MY BUS! GET OFF MY BUS!" As silly as it all seemed, no one dared laugh, chuckle, or not take it seriously. Even though most of us could tell it was an act, we obliged every confusing and contradictory command. It would be a taste of things to come.

I rushed onto the bus and found the next available seat. The corporal at the front of the bus continued to yell at us and ordered us not to speak and look straight ahead. The bus door closed, the hydraulics hissed, and we began the silent forty-five-minute ride to Quantico. I had a window seat and noticed the Pentagon on my right; up the hill beyond it were the three spires of the Air Force Memorial. It did not take long before the concrete buildings and apartments dissolved into the rolling hills of Northern Virginia. Soon we were passing lush green vegetation of coniferous and deciduous trees in full bloom. The weather was sticky and in the mid-80s. Soon we began seeing signs for Quantico. I instinctually sat up in my seat and did my best to glance to my right through the thick trees, searching for some semblance of what awaited us.

Quantico, Virginia, is a small town, which has, over the years, been nearly swallowed by the Marine Corps Base that surrounds it on three sides. On the fourth side to the east is the Potomac River. Its history is inextricably linked to the Marines. As our bus made its way through the gate which read Marine

Corps Base Quantico, I looked for anything that might give me a better sense of where I was. We passed old warehouses and brick buildings with nothing but numbered signs on them for identification. The entire place seemed austere and from a different era. It felt like I had gone back in time to WWII; I was surprised by how understated everything was. The route seemed to go on forever, deeper and deeper into the trees, as we drove next to swamps and shallow riverbeds, which would ultimately find their way to Quantico Creek and finally the Potomac River.

The bus stopped, and the same corporal began yelling at us again to get off his bus. We spilled out onto a huge parade deck, the air noticeably thick with humidity; beads of sweat formed on my brow within seconds. What I anticipated was a drill instructor in a Smokey Bear hat screaming at us to stand on the infamous yellow footprints—my impression of the Marine Corps having been formed by movies like *Full Metal Jacket* and Thomas Ricks's book *Making the Corps*, which I had read eighteen months earlier. But I realized the things that are *not* said can have just as much of an impression as things that are. The lack of fanfare and chaos, at least so far, was deliberate.

My glasses were now completely fogged over and sweat was noticeably dripping from my face and brow. A thought flashed across my mind: *This could be a very long and uncomfortable summer.* The corporal gave us instructions about where we were to go next, but considering I had no sense of where I was, the instructions did not matter.

The first day was a blur as we shuffled from line to line, building to building, for gear issue, medical exams, and haircuts. During the next three days, we would undergo a battery of physical exams, have blood drawn, and for those who wore corrective lenses as I did, be issued the ugliest, bulkiest pair of glasses ever devised by man. They are made with thick, large, brown plastic frames with an elastic strap to go around the cranium. Both male and female candidates who require corrective lenses are forced to wear them. They are known among Marines as "birth control glasses" (BCGs), derived from the perceived impossibility that a member of the opposite sex would consider you even remotely attractive while wearing them.

Additionally, if at any time during these first three days we found ourselves waiting in a queue, which was a common occurrence, we were instructed to be silent and sit on our small camp stools and study our "knowledge." This was a small, red, pocket-sized paperback booklet we had received as part of our gear issue. It contained the eleven leadership principles, fourteen leadership traits, eleven general orders, and the maximum effective range of an M-16, among other minutiae. We were to memorize it. If OCS begins the indoctrination of the individual into the Marine Corps, this little red booklet would serve as our bible for the next ten weeks.

After evening chow, we were ushered into a large auditorium— the air, which was ten degrees cooler, was refreshing. At first, there were a few speakers from the medical staff lecturing us about drinking water and hydration, as well as the importance of good hygiene throughout the summer. But as the hour crept later and later into the evening, there were fewer and fewer speakers. We remained in our seats. I was already exhausted from broken sleep, a day spent marching in the hot sun, and being disoriented from lack of schedule or timelines.

We passed the time by marking our gear, writing out last names on nearly everything we had—never deviating from the detailed instructions found in our little red booklets. It was after midnight. My group was then led back across the parade deck to our squad bay, where I thought we might get at least an hour to rest. Inside the squad bay, it appeared as if I had stepped back in time. There were old bunk beds with wall lockers in between them, and large footlockers we would share with our rack mate at the foot of each bunk. They all seemed to be at least a generation older than me. Everything was in its place. The bunks were bare and had no linens on them.

Standing at the foot of the bunk beds, we formed two lines facing each other down the length of the squad bay as the corporal walked up and down between us, saying in a loud stern voice that we would retrieve all of the linens and then turn to making our beds. Just then, across from me, on my right, I watched a candidate faint—his body hitting the linoleum floor with a heavy thud. At first, no one said a word. Then a prior-enlisted candidate got the corporal's attention. Another candidate from the far left end of the squad bay spoke up, "This candidate is an EMT and can offer some assistance."

"Get over here!" yelled the corporal. The candidate who had fainted was resuscitated and given water. Within minutes he was escorted out, and immediately dropped from OCS. I never saw him again. By now it was 03:00 and instead of being allowed to sleep in these beds, we learned how to put linens on them and make them in proper Marine Corps tradition. If it was not right and did not meet the corporal's standards, we had to remove all the linens and start over. We were then told to find a rack—it did not matter which one—and unload our gear onto it. The corporal ordered us to continue to mark our gear. We sat in silence—all fifty of us—marking our gear, doing our best to stay awake. At 05:30 we were marched to chow, after which we returned to the squad bay and were told to change into green-on-green physical training (PT) gear with our "go-fasters" (running shoes). We would be running our first physical fitness test (PFT) on no sleep and a full stomach. Thus began my second day.

On the last of these three introductory days, we were given haircuts—the final step to make all of us look the same. After our haircuts, we changed into our woodland camouflage uniforms or "cammies." While they lacked the "U.S. Marines" name tape above the left breast pocket and had only a piece of white athletic tape with our last names stenciled on them in black marker above the right, my civilian identity was now all but erased.

I glanced in the mirror at the man staring back at me. He had a bald white head, hideous eyeglasses, and was wearing camouflage. I did not recognize him. The Marine Corps was removing any remnant of individuality in each of us—the same clothes, the same haircuts, the same eyeglasses (for those who needed them), no jewelry, and no access to our cell phones. In less than seventy-two hours, we had been stripped of all the trappings of our civilian lives in order to begin behaving as members of a cohesive, collaborative military unit. Even our speech was regulated and made uniform. We were no longer allowed to use the pronoun "I." Instead, we would each refer to ourselves and each other in the third person: "this candidate" or "Candidate [last name]." The intent was to remove our selfishness and self-seeking behavior by forbidding any reference to the self.

This was the first dramatic shift in my thinking after graduating law school. For the previous three years I had been immersed in an environment composed entirely of self-interested people. Moreover, the environment encouraged it and cultivated it. Now, as I had been warned by my OSO, I would be evaluated on whether I was a team player and whether I would be willing to put others before myself. Selfishness is an easy trait to spot when misery is forced upon all. The Marine Corps applies that misery through OCS and then lets nature take its course. Any attempts by those who proudly wanted to be first in accomplishing a task, or get the most attention for doing something the right way, would often have the opposite effect by bringing negative attention to themselves and drawing the ire of the staff. In other words, individualism would be snuffed out and eradicated. Those who might persist in these behaviors would eventually be discovered, scrutinized, and if they did not change their ways, be dropped from OCS. This would be an entirely different experience than law school.

Chapter 6

PAIN

"Know that one day your pain will become your cure."

—RUMI

After all gear had been issued, initial physical fitness tests run, and the batteries of medical exams conducted during the first seventy-two hours in Quantico, on what was now the fourth day, we were led to the auditorium after morning chow. The Commanding Officer of OCS would be giving us our final brief before we were turned over to his staff. The colonel himself had been an honor graduate of OCS and had spent his entire life in the Marine Corps. I later learned that under his tenure, more candidates had been dropped by him and his staff than under any previous commander. He was known to be a draconian disciplinarian and seemingly made it his mission to attrit candidates with an exacting and extremely demanding physical fitness regimen throughout the entire evolution of OCS.

He stood solemnly on the stage in the auditorium as he addressed us. "I want you all to know that for the next ten weeks, you will experience pain. It is not personal. It is simply my business to ensure that the men and women who graduate from this school have demonstrated those qualities of intellect, discipline, and moral character which will enable them to inspire and control a group of people successfully: to be leaders. We are currently involved in two theatres of war where each of you will end up. A candidate's bearing and presence under pressure is an excellent indicator of how he or she will act under similar circumstances like combat. At OCS, we are screening all of you to determine who can perform under stress, and we will do this in many ways. You will intimately learn this in just a little while." He did not mince words, and you could tell by his stern voice he was absolutely serious about his mission in life.

I paid close attention as he introduced the staff of 4th Platoon. The enlisted drill instructors (DIs) walked out onto the stage in sharp, perfect, unison. Their uniforms crisp, campaign covers tilted so high we were unable to see their eyes, the sleeves of their camouflage blouses rolled perfectly. They looked extremely intimidating. The staff who would be training us day and night had already proven their success on the drill fields of Parris Island and Marine Corps Recruit Depot San Diego. After successful tours as Recruit Depot DIs, they had been chosen by the Marine Corps to screen and evaluate officer candidates. After he finished his introductions, the commanding officer asked one final question: "Does anyone here want to walk out right now?" No one moved. Then his final words to his staff changed my life forever: "Take charge and carry out the plan of the day."

Then, as if a pack of wild dogs had just been loosed upon all of us, the entire enlisted staff launched into a frenzy, coming at us from all sides of the auditorium. I leaped out of my seat having no idea where to go or what to do. We were told to return to our squad bay and retrieve our belongings. We sprinted back across the parade deck surging with adrenaline.

When I got to the squad bay, sweat pouring down my face, I frantically took everything out of my locker, stuffed it into my sea bag and nylon laundry bag and stood "on line" at the foot of the bunks with the rest of my platoon, arms full of gear. Then we heard the menacing sound of incomprehensible screaming and yelling coming towards us. We were to get back outside and onto the parade deck. We ran outside. Everything was chaos.

By now, all the other platoons were also on the parade deck, their belongings being dumped onto the ground. My staff took roll call, for accountability, each of us shouting, "Here, Staff Sergeant!"—our arms burning from carrying all our gear.

"Now dump all of your gear! RIGHT NOW! DUMP IT OUT. DUMP IT OUT!" They would deliberately kick our things across the parade deck as they walked by sizing up their new platoon to see if anyone dared make eye contact. "Are you bird-doggin' me, candidate?! Did I say you could look at me?"

"No, Staff Sergeant!" I yelled.

"You've got 10-9-8-7654321 to pick it up!" We now had to put everything back in. "YOU'RE NOT MOVING FAST ENOUGH, CANDIDATE!"

The platoons were so close to one another on the parade deck it was impossible to determine which platoon's staff was shouting and giving commands at whom. Someone's canister of talcum powder fell onto the parade deck, partially open, and with a swift boot-kick one of the DIs launched it thirty feet across the parade deck, spewing white powder everywhere as it spun around before coming to a rest.

Socks, shirts, underwear, shoes, books, notebook paper, everyone's belongings were scattered all over the place, but we did not dare move until given a command. We stood there helpless as our personal belongings went in every direction. The staff instructed us to pick up our sea bags. They then ordered us to find an incredibly obscure item—a pencil—and put it into the bag; it was impossible, given the chaos on the ground, to find an item that small in such a short amount of time. Then another item. And then another. "NOW DUMP IT OUT! NOW PICK IT UP! YOU'RE NOT MOVING FAST ENOUGH!"

The DIs were circling us and weaving in and out of our ranks in order to prey upon their next unsuspecting victims and no one was safe. While one was giving us commands to find a particular item, the others from other platoons suddenly appeared on our left or right, screaming in our faces that we had retrieved the wrong item or we weren't moving fast enough (and no one ever did), their spittle landing on our faces. "WHAT ARE YOU DOING, CANDIDATE?! Don't you know the difference between your left and your right?!" This continued for some time. Then we were instructed to go back into the squad bay with all of our belongings. "Now pick up your freakin' trash! You've got 10-9-8-765432…1!"

I grabbed whatever I could and stuffed it into my sea bag and laundry bag, nervous about what would happen to me when the DI got to one. Thankfully, all of my things were in close proximity to where I had been standing, but others were not so lucky. Some things were more than twenty yards away with another platoon's gear—maybe it was a uniform blouse or a polo shirt, maybe it was a tennis shoe, or the stencils and shoe polish needed to mark gear. It did not matter, nothing was our own anymore, we would spend the night sifting through whatever was in our bags trying to retrieve our original items and help others find theirs.

I ran back to the squad bay where the madness continued. And now that we were inside a confined space, I could tell just how loud our staff was yelling. Everything inside the squad bay was fair game for being tossed—our footlockers, our wall lockers, and our bunks. The DIs relentlessly caused havoc and disorder wherever they went, and they had only just begun to make good on the colonel's promise.

OCS is not "officer boot camp." Unlike Marine enlisted recruits who, once their training has begun, must ultimately graduate boot camp, even if it means being recycled to subsequent training companies, the Marine Corps treats officer candidates differently—it screens them. This means there is potential for either medical disqualification, being dropped, or dropping on request (DOR).

Despite the different paradigm for OCS and what the Marine Corps is evaluating in its candidates, the staff were no less inclined to dilute their raw aggression. They were the most rabid, high-intensity group of people I had ever seen. Legendary in their intimidation, draconian discipline, and volcanic tempers, nothing in the world can compare to a Marine Corps DI screaming in your face. The simplest of their demands may go unheeded by a completely shocked candidate who has no idea how to react to such unalloyed aggression and animation. They are unlike any other group of people you will ever meet—and for the next ten weeks, they would rule our lives.

Very little of OCS focuses on the "art and science" of warfighting—candidates must first learn how to become part of a unit before that unit can be expected to achieve a goal or a mission. Likewise, we learned very little by way of tactics or field craft. Due to it being a screening process, the Marine Corps, in a relatively short amount of time, must apply certain kinds of pressure and friction on its officer candidates in order to determine whether they possess the requisite attributes or potential to be a leader of Marines. Therefore, OCS is a grueling summer of carefully applied stress.

The staff applied stress in several ways: first, the incessant high-intensity yelling and screaming by the DIs. Even when the screaming is not being directed at you, one is still on high alert because it could rain down on you at a moment's notice. And when it is directed at you, your muscles tighten, endorphins are released, and like a teapot slowly coming to a boil, the stress mounts, little by little, hour by hour. These undulations of low-stress and high-stress begin to sap your body of energy.

Second, and what is more commonly the culprit, OCS puts a premium on the physical fitness of officer candidates. The hallmark of being a Marine officer is being physically fit. The Marine Corps understands that when a young lieutenant stands before his platoon, although ranking highest, the lieutenant will also have the least amount of experience of all the platoon members. So in order to garner the immediate respect of his subordinates, every Marine officer must be in excellent physical condition. His stamina, drive, and perseverance need to outlast the men he is leading. Known among officer candidates as the "summer of 300," from June to August, we would run more than 300 miles—an average of about five miles a day—throughout the hills of Quantico with temperatures in the mid-90s and the air thick with humidity in conditions that can only be described as a wet oven. But running was only part of the physical fitness regimen. Sprinkled throughout every PT session were calisthenics of all kinds, push-ups, pull-ups, crunches, the obstacle course, and the endurance course.

Stress was applied a third way because every day was something new and unexpected—not only insofar as what would be asked of us, but the order or schedule of events was relatively unknown. The rationale being that a certain peace of mind or even complacency can set in if one knows or is able to anticipate what is coming next, and with that can come a certain sense of control. When a person is unaware of how long he will be doing something—especially something strenuous and painful—instead of being able to relax knowing that whatever is causing the pain will be over soon enough, the mind struggles to remain focused. In combat you will never know when your next respite is coming, so the Marine Corps does not train that way. This particular technique is remarkable at revealing how an individual will behave in a similar circumstance, and how calm he or she can remain during seemingly interminable painful circumstances. I am absolutely convinced that if you want to see someone's true character, take away his comforts and deprive him of sleep. In an effort to strip everything away from us to see how well or poorly we might react, the Marine Corps surgically applied stress and fatigue on all of us by keeping the candidate from knowing future events. This was a trend that I realized was part of the Marine Corps training paradigm *in toto*, and one I would poignantly learn during Infantry Officer Course.

In addition to the PT regimen, there is the academic evaluation of OCS. While there is nothing particularly intellectually difficult about the academics and basic knowledge we were accountable for, it was the saturation of the schedule and having no designated time to study the information that was a stress-multiplier. The teaching style was formulaic and almost nothing was offered up for discussion or debate. This was in stark contrast to the seemingly interminable law school debates. We would be evaluated throughout the summer on our mastery of these subjects. But more than the academic evaluations, or even being able to respond immediately to a DI's impromptu quiz on the parade deck, memorizing these pieces of information made them automatic, and—most importantly—made them part of each of us. The intent being that we would slowly begin to identify with the leadership traits of: judgment, justice, dependability, integrity, decisiveness, tact, initiative, enthusiasm, bearing, unselfishness, courage, knowledge, leadership, and endurance. Amid the storm of daily activity, it would be essential to recite silently to oneself a small body of knowledge by memory—in line for the chow hall, during PT runs, or while cleaning one's rifle. Or if one had the stamina after "lights out."

Most nights before lights out, the DIs and Navy corpsman would walk down the squad bay and conduct a superficial inspection of our bodies. We would be wearing the black nylon and foam "flip-flops" and green skivvy shorts, but we were told to remove our green t-shirts. To hasten the process, once inspected by the corpsman, we would then inspect one another. We were looking for blisters, ticks, abrasions, and anything out of the ordinary. Our bodies' constant contact with dirt, germs, bacteria, and sweat—our own and others'—made us especially susceptible to a dangerous bacteria called *cellulitis*. Cellulitis presents as a patch of red skin or pustule causing inflammation, which usually includes redness, warmth, pain, and swelling. It is particularly aggressive, and while it might only affect the skin's surface, it might also affect subcutaneous tissues and/or spread to your lymph nodes and bloodstream. During the first class in the auditorium on the day we had arrived, we were lectured on the importance of personal hygiene, and cellulitis was the topic used to drive home its importance. We were shown pictures of the worst-case scenarios as a result of ignoring the symptoms.

I say ignore because the Marine Corps tends to draw men and women not easily deflected from their goals. Officer candidates often possess formidable resolve and will suffer through excruciating pain, propelled by the unwavering intensity of their desire to earn the title *Marine*. The thought of being dropped or starting over is worse than enduring any physical agony. It is precisely this attitude of perseverance the Marine Corps wants in its ranks. Unfortunately, the sort of individuals who are programmed to ignore physical ailments and distress and keep pushing themselves may also disregard signs of real or imminent danger. This forms a dilemma for any candidate who finds himself in physical pain or severely ill. In order to graduate, you must be exceedingly driven, but if you are too driven and ignore symptoms, you may suffer an irreparable medical setback and be medically disqualified. The danger the staff tries to mitigate comes from candidates who do not report physical ailments for fear of calling attention to themselves, being put on light duty, or worse yet, being dropped for medical purposes. But left untreated, cellulitis and other ailments can become life-threatening.

Then there was the "crud." This was a constant, hacking cough that nearly every candidate experienced at one time or another during OCS. It was a result of people, who have come from all over the country, suddenly living in very close quarters, exchanging germs and sweat, who are constantly dirty and sleep-deprived—the crud is unavoidable. It does not appear until about three weeks into the training schedule, at a time when our immune systems have been worn down and are no longer as resilient as they were when we first arrived. Our bodies having succumbed to the ever-present fatigue—we all had some varying degree of the crud. The worst case in my platoon developed pneumonia. The candidate had been given three days of light duty, which meant he would not be required to do the same activities as the rest of us. But if after those three days he was unable to maintain the tempo and demands of the daily routine, he would be dropped. To his credit, he pushed through it and continued to train and ultimately graduated. There were similar stories of several candidates suffering twisted ankles, knees, and other small joint injuries, astonishingly grotesque foot blisters, and sunburn.

As long as the candidate did not complain or ask to be sent to medical, he was allowed to continue training, unless of course, these nightly inspections by the staff and corpsmen revealed an urgent medical issue. Thus, another part of the calculus of these nightly inspections was to see how badly candidates wanted the title Marine—almost all injuries were suffered in silence. We had to become comfortable with a new normal of physical and mental stress.

After "lights out" there was still work to be done, gear to be repaired, and laundry to be washed. No matter how soiled our uniforms and boots had become from that day's training, we were responsible for ensuring they looked like new the next day. This was always the great dilemma: no matter how clean I get my uniform tonight, tomorrow it will get dirty and will need to be washed again. Do I remain awake cleaning and repairing my gear? Do I study? Or do I sleep?

Chapter 7

———

A NEW IDENTITY

"The more important an activity is to your soul's evolution, the more resistance you will feel."

—STEVEN PRESSFIELD, *DO THE WORK*

The method used to reveal any selfish individuality, failure to adapt, or failure to become part of a cohesive unit is close order drill. Tracing its roots all the way back to Sumer and ancient Egypt, down through the Romans, drill was a response to the need to assemble and move large groups of men on the battlefield. Modern drill consists of two types: close order drill and extended or "combat" drill. Close order drill teaches the formal movements and formations used in marching, parades, and ceremonies and is an essential foundation for combat drill to maintain cohesion on a chaotic battlefield. At its core, drill keeps individuals in unison to function as a complete whole. It does this by accentuating the natural rhythm and beat of walking or marching, "Left…left…left, right…left," and it is made all the more emphatic by the DI's strong cadence. Most importantly, it develops a sense of teamwork, discipline, and self-control; promoting automatic performance of duties and immediate obedience to orders under stressful circumstances. It cultivates instinctive responses to the control of leaders.

What close order drill does not reveal is leadership potential and decisive problem-solving. On the very best day, I was only average at drill, and it showed. Even minor missteps and miscounts were considered egregious errors, which sent our DIs into a frenzy as they berated all culprits with some of the most heinous and hilarious verbal tirades. They forced us to repeat the maneuver over and over with ass-bleeding detail in order to get it right.

The problem was, my law school blood was still in me. Hence, a vicious cycle was at play for me: *an insecure ego preoccupied with performance.* This led to stress; stress was a distractor, and distraction led to mistakes. These mistakes brought down a reign of terror from the senior DI, which, in turn, made me more anxious, and the terrible cycle would start anew. The two DIs had my number. I began to wonder if the second purpose of close order drill—to weed out the individual—would eventually claim me as a casualty, particularly when it came to my first rifle inspection.

A rifle inspection demonstrates the candidate's comfort and proficiency with his rifle. It also reveals how well he pays attention to the details of a clean weapon system, down to the smallest component of the entire weapon. Ultimately, I had to demonstrate that my weapon was functional. The final movement of this demonstration is to press down on the trigger with the left thumb. In all other circumstances throughout the summer we would keep our weapons on "safe," the mechanism which locks the trigger and prevents it from being pressed. Before inspection arms, however, we would switch the safety "off" so the trigger would pull. I had failed to do this. So when I pressed down on the trigger, nothing happened. A surge of adrenaline shot through me. There was no hiding my error. I fidgeted with my weapon as quickly as I could in order to switch the weapon off "safe" and complete inspection arms—by now I was well outside the sharp, crisp, deliberate movements of any inspection. When I finished, the DI's eyes were as big as golf balls, incredulous as to what he had just witnessed. Without taking his eyes off me: "Scribe!" he said to the candidate who followed in trace of the DI to record any errors. "Write this down—inspection arms equals abortion!"

My embarrassment and insecurity were astronomical. He snatched my weapon from me and began his inspection—all was lost. My error had now opened the door for extreme scrutiny of my weapon and my person by the DI. No matter how clean I thought it was before the inspection began, due to my mistake, it was now impossible for my rifle to get a "clean bill of health."

"Excessive CLP on the bolt. Too much CLP on the charging handle. God damn, Candidate Pavlak! Did you even clean your weapon?!"

(I had cleaned every inch of it, but it did not matter.) "Yes, Staff Sergeant."

"Well, I disagree. Are you calling me a liar?!"

"No, Staff Sergeant!"

"Scribe! Dirt on the butt-stock. Rust on the magazine-well. Rust on the flash suppressor."

During most inspections even one oversight or error is bad. I now had a litany of them. Each one the DI listed made my spirit sink a little more. He gave my rifle back to me with a look of disgust. "You better fix yourself, Pavlak, because that was one of the worst things I've ever seen! Do you even want to be here, candidate?!" He said this with almost no fanfare or emotion as he moved on to the next candidate in formation.

I was rattled. Just when I thought I was making progress, I committed several egregious errors in less than two minutes. For me and for anyone else, yesterday's performance did not matter. After my inspection, while the DI made his way through the rest of the platoon, I considered what my law school friends might be doing—writing briefs, meeting with clients, making arguments—and I wondered if I had made the right decision by attending OCS. That night after lights out, despite my fatigue, that day's events had me unsettled and I could not sleep.

As I considered my pathetic performance during the inspection I realized graduating from law school meant nothing without passing the Bar, and I had no guarantee of graduating from OCS. I went to my footlocker and retrieved a book I had brought from home: *The Strenuous Life* by Theodore Roosevelt. Of all the books I could have taken with me, I chose to bring the indomitable spirit of T.R., which, only a few months earlier, had helped me cope with the devastation of failing the Bar exam. In the wake of my failure, I memorized his famous passage of "The Man in the Arena," taking particular solace in the words, "The credit belongs to the man who is actually in the arena, whose face is marred by dust and sweat and blood; who strives valiantly; who errs, and comes short again and again, because there is no effort without error and shortcoming[...]"[13]

Now, in the enterprise of attempting to become a Marine Officer, I knew it would be important to maintain perspective and persevere despite obstacles. I leafed through the pages stopping at another passage I had read several times before and went to the portion I had underlined:

> Perhaps there is no more important component of character than steadfast resolution. The boy who is going to make a great man, or is going to count in any way in after life, must make up his mind not merely to overcome a thousand obstacles, but to win in spite of a thousand repulses or defeats. He may be able to wrest success along the lines on which he originally started. He may have to try something entirely new. On the one hand, he must not be volatile and irresolute, and, on the other hand, he must not fear to try a new line because he has failed in another.[14]

I realized I wanted to be a Marine more than I had ever wanted anything else in my life, including being a lawyer. My road of trials had begun with my encounter with my own hubris, something I had subconsciously been harboring since law school—not in spite of it, but precisely because of it. It had come from thinking myself good enough to be a Marine simply because I had made it to OCS. I had come to Quantico with a deranged notion that whatever came my way, I would be able to make it through. I was now facing a challenge I had never

---

13   "Theodore Roosevelt's Citizenship in a Republic: The Man in the Arena," Leadership Now, accessed August 29, 2022, https://www.leadershipnow.com/tr-citizenship.html.

14   Theodore Roosevelt, *The Strenuous Life: Essays and Addresses* (New York: Cosimo Classics Publishing, 2006), 119.

encountered before—one that hard work alone could not overcome and one that certainly didn't care that I had graduated from law school. My arrogance had been laid bare on the drill field. Hard work would not be enough, desire would not be enough, and effort did not matter.

As I closed the book, I read an email I had received from Nate Fick, which I taped to its inside cover. Before I left for OCS, I had read Nate Fick's book *One Bullet Away: The Making of A Marine Officer*, which galvanized my desire to become a Marine. I had written Nate to both thank and congratulate him for writing it. I told him I would be going to OCS that summer and asked him for some advice about making it through to graduation:

```
Chris,

Three things:

1. The goal is to graduate, not necessarily to
   graduate ranked first in your class. So take it
   easy on the obstacle course and don't wrench your
   knee while trying to break the course record.
   Finish, and finish strong, but don't go down in
   flames while trying to finish first.

2. Remember that OCS ain't the real Corps. Just
   keep your head down, do as you're told, and don't
   question the rules. Graduate, and then get on
   with your life.

3. Always, always, always put your platoon-mates
   first. Take care of them, and they'll take
   care of you. Also, the staff will notice your
   attitude.

Good luck, and Semper Fi

Nate Fick
```

As I read the email, Nate's advice hit home. I would need to be much more than just a hardworking individual. I realized what I was missing was any appreciation for the men around me who were trying just as hard as I was, perhaps harder. I would need to exercise humility, stop competing with the other candidates, and most of all, stop competing with myself and my own ego. Schadenfreude must give way to esprit de corps.

I made it through that period of OCS by changing my attitude and not allowing the small things, "the committee" as I have called it, to hold court inside my head. It was an exercise in not allowing perfection to get in the way of the good. We were more than halfway through OCS and after this, I noticed for the first time, I stopped caring about being perfect.

There are four evolutions of training which accentuate the small-unit leadership skills the Marine Corps seeks from its Officers. First would come Leadership Reaction Course (LRC I and II), then Small-Unit Leadership Exercise (SULE I & II), the latter being the culminating evolution before graduation. The Leadership Reaction course is an evolution designed to test candidates as fire team leaders. In each evolution, the candidate will be given an almost "no-win" problem they have to negotiate with time constraints and very limited equipment. The evaluation criteria are: bias for action, confidence, decisiveness, bearing, and ability to communicate the plan to one's peers. Success did not mean achieving the objective—many of the problems are nearly impossible given the objective, time, and resources each team has. The important thing is to stay out of your own head, think clearly, work as a team, develop simple plans—and be decisive. The problems require quick thinking, decisiveness, a distribution of work, and most importantly, teamwork.

One cannot become fixated on finding the silver bullet to a problem, because rarely will such a situation present itself in combat. Just as important are any selfish attitudes a candidate may exhibit when stressed. The "I'll-just-do-it-myself" attitude is also a guarantee of receiving a poor evaluation. It is important to rely on the team you are leading, trust them to execute the plan and think for themselves when dealing with friction. Success will be based on whether or not the fire team leader conveyed his intent to the rest of the team, so when presented with friction and in the absence of orders, they can still execute, and ultimately accomplish the mission. We would be evaluated on whether we were demonstrating and personifying the leadership traits and principles that nearly two months earlier we had simply recited from memory.

There are two evolutions which serve as the bookends of this phase: Small Unit Leadership Exercise I and II also known as SULE I and SULE II. (pronounced "soo-lee"), which are identical in design, but different in execution. SULE I is executed in week six, SULE II, week nine. These two evolutions revealed to the staff what no other evolution up to that point had: leading a group of ten to fifteen peers, performing under pressure, fighting through fatigue, and persevering through friction and uncertainty—all in one long evolution.

Reveille for SULE II was at 02:00. We were to be in platoon formation in thirty minutes on the parade deck with our gear and our weapons. We were in the chow hall by 03:00 attempting to consume as many calories as possible for the long day ahead. We were then broken into squads of ten to fifteen candidates each, made up mostly of the peers in my platoon, but one or two were from different platoons.

Each of us carried our weapon, several magazines of blank rounds, wore an FLC, a waist belt with two canteens of water, our patrol packs with extra socks, two Meals-Ready-to-Eat (MREs), and a CamelBak full of water. More important than conserving food was conserving water and drinking it responsibly throughout the day. A misstep resulting in a twisted ankle or hyper-extended knee, or aggravating an injury from earlier in the summer may result in being medically dropped with only a week left before graduation. A medical problem would likely mean starting OCS all over again from the beginning once the body healed and the next OCS class picked up—something none of us even wanted to imagine.

We would operate as an autonomous squad throughout the day with no direct supervision from the staff. We had been living and working together long enough to know what right looked like, and now it was up to us to demonstrate how much we had really learned about motivation, bias for action, time management, endurance, and teamwork. We took accountability just as the first rays of sunlight were visible in the sky. The sergeant, who had a radio, would be waiting for the command to begin. Each mission would last between thirty and forty-five minutes. We would be operating as a squad all day, and there would be no DIs. And from this point on there would be no motorized transportation; we would be moving on foot between different stations. Time would have priority. Once arriving at the new station the new squad leader would take over, receive an order from the new evaluator, develop a plan, deliver an order to the squad, and execute the mission. Paramount to our individual success would be remembering all of the things we had learned throughout the summer and, most importantly, leading our peers as a team.

One challenge of leading people is demanding they do the right thing despite any additional work, friction, endurance, or pain it requires. This is especially difficult when everyone is the same rank—or, as in our case, has no rank. Finally, as fatigue sets in and makes even the simple things difficult, people's true colors are revealed. The wisdom of OCS is in immersing the candidate into situations with several variables—some they can control and many they cannot—all under the auspices of the mission being the most important. This presses upon the candidate the importance of remaining calm, thinking through the friction, and employing the leadership techniques he has learned.

Given the fallibility of the human mind in stressful and chaotic situations when sleep might be in short supply, the five-paragraph order is the basic planning checklist to ensure the commander has accounted for elements (and sub-elements) of a tactical plan. The components of the order were drilled into us from the first day we opened our red books of knowledge: Situation, Mission, Execution, Administration and Logistics, and Command and Signal. The acronym "SMEAC" was something we kept at the tip of our tongues throughout the summer, anticipating a DI's on-the-spot questioning. Likewise, during SULE I and SULE II, it is imperative that a candidate know two things: the five-paragraph OPORDER and the Mission. For example, if a mission is to deliver supplies to a nearby friendly position, performing that tactical task is paramount. As the squad is patrolling in order to make the resupply, it takes contact from an enemy. The patrol leader decides to orient on the enemy, engage, and assault through his battle position. Many candidates might assume they are successful. They put the squad in a consolidated 360 position and take reports from the fire team leaders. The squad leader approaches the instructor, gets on one knee, and confidently gives a full report knowing that the enemy was destroyed. The evaluator tells the squad leader they just failed SULE. The mission was to deliver the ammunition.

The sergeant who was evaluating us received word over the radio that we could begin. Because I happened to be serving as the candidate platoon squad leader at the beginning of SULE II, he indicated I would be going first. I designated who the fire team leaders were and instructed them to assign candidates to post security. I then departed with the evaluator to receive my order. As he began to use the five-paragraph order in SMEAC format (Situation, Mission, Execution, Administration and Logistics, and Command and Signal), I jotted down everything I could into a formatted template, concentrating on the details, determined to be able to communicate my order succinctly to the rest of the squad. We would be conducting an assault on-line, penetrating the enemy defenses, and regrouping on the far side of the defensive position. I delivered my version of SMEAC to the squad and gave my fire team leaders the tasks I wanted accomplished. We stepped off at 06:20.

Everything went according to plan. When we encountered the enemy the squad followed the tasks I had given at the terrain model. We pushed through the enemy's position and regrouped on the other side in a consolidated 360 position. I took accountability ensuring we had all the candidates we started with, then inspected for any injuries and the amount of remaining ammunition. I turned and gave the full report to the sergeant evaluator who said, "OK, well done." And just like that my mission was over. He pulled me aside to give me a five-minute breakdown of how my mission went, what I did correctly, and what I did not do correctly. That was it. Now it was someone else's turn. For the remainder of the day, as the humidity and temperatures soared, we would be working together to solve the problems and accomplish the missions of each squad leader throughout the training area.

A Marine rifle squad, and nearly any military unit, will respond to a leader who, despite missing some detail, is decisive in his planning and delivers his orders firmly and confidently. Throughout the day we would do more than fifty buddy-rushes, evacuate casualties, carry ammo cans, sprint up and down the harsh terrain, and repeat. As we became more and more fatigued, firm and simple orders would resonate the most with the squad. Throughout all of it, we became a well-oiled machine, and instead of fifteen personalities, we became a cohesive and cooperative group.

As each squad staggered into a staging area following the all-day event, some hobbled because of blistered feet or twisted ankles, others nibbled on portions of their MREs, some sat quietly staring in the middle-distance exhausted, while still others had amazing amounts of energy and were shouting motivational "ooh-rahs" and giving high-fives to each candidate who lumbered into our staging area. OCS was, for all intents and purposes, over. I would be graduating in three days. We had one final inspection in our Service Alpha uniforms before we prepared for our graduation ceremony scheduled for August 10.

Graduating from OCS does not make a candidate a Marine. In order to achieve the title, one must be commissioned and take the Marine Officer's Oath. Accordingly, after the graduation ceremony on the parade deck in front of friends and family, we hurried back to our squad-bays, and all those who would be commissioned changed into their Service "A's" and loaded buses to go to the National Museum of the Marine Corps in Quantico, only two miles away. After the guest speaker, we were all instructed to stand, raise our right hands, and take the Oath. Time slowed as I spoke every word. Our DIs masked their pride with looks of contempt, insinuating we still really were not good enough to call ourselves Marine officers. What struck me was, despite screaming at me only two days earlier, they were now addressing me as "sir." The blur of the previous ten weeks crystallized as these enlisted Marines, who had worked tirelessly to train us, were now saluting us. It was a humbling experience.

I had been so fixated on doing things the right way, not skylining myself by making an egregious error, and trying to recover from the mistakes I had made on the drill field halfway through, that at first I didn't notice any transformative change in myself. But reflecting on the experience in hindsight, I now know it was the beginning. Graduating from OCS helped stop the cycle of self-deprecation I had been repeating to myself since October 2006. And for the first time in a long time—perhaps in my life—I had unwavering pride in what I had achieved and could truly call my own—nothing short of a new identity. It would be another nine months before I realized the scope and scale of my transformation.

Charlie Company, 4th Platoon at Marine Officer Candidates School in Quantico, Virginia in the summer of 2007. I'm in the middle of the fifth row. (U.S. Marine Corps)

Chapter 8

FROZEN FOX

"You cannot exaggerate about the Marines. They are convinced to the point of arrogance, that they are the most ferocious fighters on earth—and the amusing thing about it is that they are."
—FATHER KEVIN KEANEY, U.S. NAVY CHAPLAIN
WHO SERVED WITH MARINES IN KOREA

Almost all of us who had graduated from OCS two weeks earlier would pick up with Fox Company at the end of August; other companies, which had begun a few calendar months ahead of us, were already well underway in their training cycle. Alpha Company had graduated in June, Bravo in July, Charlie had approximately three months to go, and so on. Then there was "Frozen Fox" because the bulk of our Field Exercises or "FEXs" (where we would spend entire weeks in the field) would be taking place during December, January, and February. Fox Company had six platoons, each with approximately forty Marines in them. Each platoon was led by a captain who was a staff platoon commander (SPC). These captains demonstrated such exceptional service while platoon commanders (or in equivalent junior leadership or staff positions in the fleet) that they had been personally selected by the Marine Corps to be exemplars of leadership for us, the newest batch of leaders in the Marine Corps.

The Basic School (TBS) training area, known as Camp Barrett, occupies nearly all of Marine Corps Base Quantico on the western side of the I-95 corridor. However, the aesthetics leave something to be desired. The feeling was no different than what I had felt riding the bus through the gates to OCS. Sprinkled throughout Camp Barrett were dormitories, classrooms, a pool, an armory, and huge fields, which I soon learned doubled as helicopter landing zones. We saw other companies of lieutenants hurrying to and from class with backpacks, water bottles, and coffee mugs.

Besides its ethos and mystique, one of the hallmarks of the Marine Corps is how it trains its officers. Unlike the other branches of service, the Marine Corps requires all of its officers—whether they are ground officers, pilots, or lawyers—to have a basic working knowledge and understanding of leading a Marine rifle platoon. TBS is a six-month-long immersion into all things infantry for the newly minted Marine lieutenant, cultivating a uniform understanding of infantry tactics spanning the entire officer corps. As a byproduct, regardless of occupational specialty, every Marine officer graduates TBS well-versed in basic infantry tactics, so that no matter what the officer's eventual military occupational specialty (MOS) is, he or she will have an appreciation for the unique difficulties and friction of being an infantryman for the rest of his or her career. Likewise, TBS is where the fraternal camaraderie of Marine officers begins.

TBS evaluates its students in three categories: leadership, academics, and military skills. However, oftentimes all three categories are combined into a single evolution or period of instruction. First we sat through lectures on the subject matter. The subsequent week was our practical application in the field of the things we had learned in the classroom. It was during these FEXs where we were scrutinized on our leadership abilities to be decisive and lead our platoons against competing interests, our mastery of the substantive subject matter, and its real-world application in the field. Everything we did—from land navigation, to marksmanship, to logistics, to fire and movement—was galvanized through practical application and then tested in the classroom.

I moved my gear to a room down the corridor of the building that fifth platoon would occupy. When I entered the room, I noticed the bottom bunk already had gear on it; other than two chairs, another bed, a wardrobe, and a desk, the room was empty, so I took the top bunk. I brushed my teeth, washed my face, and went to sleep without even putting sheets on my bed.

When I awoke the next morning, I climbed down and stepped on the mattress of the bed beneath mine. I realized the room's occupant had returned after I had fallen asleep and my climb down had woken him up. "Oh, sorry man; hope I didn't wake you," I said.

"No worries," he replied as he put his glasses on, still in the dark.

I introduced myself. "I'm Chris."

"Tim. You wanna get some coffee in a bit?" he asked.

"Sure, just let me brush my teeth and get dressed."

"Same," he replied. Over coffee we swapped stories of our experiences of OCS over the summer; we had both been in Charlie Company, he in 3rd Platoon, I in 4th.

Tim grew up in Santa Monica, California, an only child. He had studied philosophy at UCLA and had been editor of the UCLA newspaper. Before OCS, he had finished a two-year assignment in New York City with Teach for America. I had no way of knowing at the time how randomly choosing the top bunk of a barracks room would be the genesis of a deep and lasting friendship with one of the best Marine officers I would ever meet. Tim's Southern California upbringing had instilled a laid-back demeanor to most everything he did—he let life come to him, but he was an equally cerebral and pensive man, able to understand information upon reading it only once with an amazing ability to recall details.

Over the next six months, many of the Marines in the platoon, including me, would come to him for his tactical savvy, easygoing demeanor, and sharp intellect. One of his many gifts was the ability to see the big picture. He intuitively knew what was worth stressing about and what was not, and for Tim, most was not. He is also an excellent storyteller.

We made a weekly ritual of breakfast at IHOP in Stafford, just outside the back gate of Camp Barrett, to discuss the highs and lows of the previous week's evolution of training. It became apparent during our weekly breakfasts that neither one of us had joined the Marine Corps because of a particular love of the outdoors, weapons, or even a naïve sense of leading men to heroism on the battlefield. Service to our country was important, but not necessarily the sole driving factor. I had joined as essentially what amounted to a "plan B" for my life. Indeed wearing a uniform, studying infantry tactics, and taking orders was the last thing I envisioned myself doing only three years earlier when I was a first-year law student. I joined because I thought my back was up against the wall and needed to escape what felt like professional claustrophobia as a result of my failures. In many ways, I considered the Marine Corps a last resort for breaking out of a paradigm, and I had nothing left to lose.

The first phase of TBS focused on marksmanship. We learned "by the numbers" the workings of the M16A4, the standard infantry rifle of the U.S. Military of the time, or the M4 Carbine, a shortened 14.5 inch (versus 20 inch M16A4) version of the M16. The M16 is a select fire (meaning fully automatic/burst) gas-operated 5.56mm weapon system accurate to point targets at 500 meters and area targets to 800 meters. The A4 version was the fourth iteration of the rifle since Vietnam, and featured rail mounting systems that allowed modular attachments of weapons systems (such as the M203 40 millimeter grenade launcher) or improvements such as visible and IR laser aiming devices. We also learned the components of the M9 pistol.

We would be taking our time "snapping in," acquiring the muscle memory of manipulating the weapon in different positions: standing, sitting, and prone; learning how to regulate our breathing; and make wind adjustments. We mustered every morning at 05:00 to make the three-mile hike to the rifle range. We would become poignantly familiar with this route for the next six months. Most memorable is that after the first half mile, the trail bends to the left and makes a sharp incline aptly named Cardiac Hill. Nearly every hike to the field and every forced march began and ended with Cardiac Hill.

I found the pedagogical approach of TBS intriguing. Law school had turned me into a selfish student, and I was taken aback by the instinctual camaraderie of my peers. For the first time in my professional adult life, I was in an environment that thrived on teamwork and the notion that we were all in this together. If a lieutenant was having difficulty learning how to convert his grid azimuth to a magnetic azimuth, learning the five stages of planning in Helo Ops, how to set up his machine guns in the defense, or a myriad of other new topics—it was almost expected that his peers help him. I was shocked. The last three years of my life were in a dog-eat-dog world of ultra-competitive and status-driven people, many of whom would do anything they could to outshine, outperform, and outdo their peers, even to the point of a comrade's downfall. Now, in TBS, as was the case during OCS, selfish attitudes were met with disdain and eventually extinguished.

I began to understand why the Marine Corps thrives on teamwork and places such a premium on esprit de corps—for the well-being of the Marine on your left and right. Safety and combat effectiveness would derive from mutually supporting each other, helping each other, and looking after the other's well-being. Likewise, it was incumbent upon those of us who did understand a certain topic to take the time and teach anyone who might not. And rarely did the same person understand all aspects of our training. It was imperative not to let ego get in the way of learning because, in a very real sense, our lives—or the lives of our Marines—might depend on our real abilities under fire, not on how smart we appeared.

As I considered the no-nonsense, but collegial academic environment cultivated at TBS, I realized some of the important aspects that had been missing from my law school experience. Law school's emphasis on individual effort, class rank, and teaching students that they are about to enter an adversarial profession lent itself to being a sterile and selfish environment. Ironically, now as I was training and preparing for real combat, the Marine Corps helped me realize there simply is no place for selfishness or ego in the profession of arms. It will get people killed. Captains were teaching us and fervently encouraging us to understand how essential teamwork is for mission accomplishment. These were men and women who, having just returned from kinetic operations, had every reason to be filled with overblown self-importance. Instead, the opposite was true.

The lectures, discussions, and conversations were starkly different from the tone of those that took place during law school. There was no unwillingness to share information for fear someone might perform better on an exam or in the field. The special ethos about the Marine Corps centered around that common loyalty of being Marines.

The pedagogical approach was simultaneously one of respect for extremely dangerous situations and of humility because they had seen firsthand the ugliness of combat and were teaching us to respect it, and respect the violence we were being trained to harness. They were doing everything they could to ensure we knew our craft. This was serious business with no margin for error. And it was this appreciation for the gravity of what we were being trained to do that I felt was missing in law school.

In law school, we had the luxury to debate *ad nauseam* any legal issue confined in a toxic environment of hyper-competition and egoism which ostensibly served no higher purpose. As law students, we could be as naïve and self-centered as we wanted because nothing else was at stake except a higher GPA. I also realized another byproduct of law school, in the form of information bias, and I was unaware it existed until I joined the Marine Corps.

TBS immerses students into situations that mimic the kinds of situations a leader will constantly encounter—fatigue, friction, incomplete information, insufficient resources to accomplish a mission, and an enemy—all of it simultaneously. While individual periods of instruction would teach us about a very specific topic (e.g., setting up a platoon in the defense), the more savvy lieutenants began to see the forest for the trees and how these basic warfighting tenets of speed, maneuver, friction, and agility were incorporated into a training evolution and manifesting themselves throughout the six months.

My problem, being a new law school graduate, and still having a chip on my shoulder for not passing the Bar exam, was that I made it my concern to get mired in the detail to know as many facts and nuances about a situation as possible—just as a lawyer would want to know everything about a case. He or she must know what facts are dispositive and which are inconsequential. A client, who might be paying $300, $500, or $1,000/hour is not satisfied with the 80 percent solution, and would certainly not tolerate the 70 percent. Lawyers need all the facts. If they don't have them, it is the attorney's job—and duty—to find them, learn them, and master them. A Marine officer does not have that luxury.

I realized my fixation on seeking details during a Tactical Decision Game (TDG). The purpose of the exercise was to quickly receive information, process it, decisively determine when I had enough information, then finally—and most importantly—develop a plan. The entire exercise only lasted fifteen minutes. A staff member read a Situation Report (SITREP), and we were free to get up and leave at any time once each of us thought he or she had enough information to write our own Fragmentary Order (FRAG-O), which we had to complete in whatever time remained of the original fifteen minutes. I waited for all the information—about twelve minutes worth—for more and more minutiae. Eventually, running out of substantive facts, the staff member seemed to go off script and even began making things up. Now, I finally felt comfortable enough to leave the room and make my own plan. The problem was I only had about two minutes and thirty seconds to do so. I didn't have enough time to write down the entire situation, let alone make a cogent plan. I realized that, given the context, law school had handicapped me with the need for as much information as possible. As a Marine, however, I would need to become comfortable with making a decision with incomplete or entirely missing information. Unsurprisingly I ran out of time devising my plan because I was biased toward wanting all of the precious information I could get. The instructor called on me. My plan was half-baked and pathetic. It wasn't a plan at all. There would be a lot of "unlearning" my law school thinking.

Our FEXs meant we would be outside from early Monday morning until Friday afternoon—enduring all of the weather and temperatures of Northern Virginia in between. As the weather deteriorated into the cold and wet winter months of Virginia, the key to staying warm would be staying dry. Once autumn came to an end around mid-November, the wet miserable cold was inescapable. The cold became friction itself.

We would normally arise at 04:30 in order to get to chow at 5:00. Then we would draw weapons from the armory. We returned to our rooms to make final adjustments to our packs, put on warming layers, and then form up outside. Tim and I would both remain inside as long as we could before stepping out into the frosty air. We cherished these last precious moments of warmth and attempted to get stoked to meet the challenges of the pervasive cold for the next five days. I would crank the volume on my speakers and play our favorite "before-going-to-the-field" song. It would become my and Tim's ritual before every FEX. Donning our warming layers, strapping on our backpacks, and gulping down the last bit of coffee, we made every attempt to warm our bodies, as the motivational music warmed our souls.

We packed everything that might offer warmth in the sub-freezing temperatures of December, January, and February in Northern Virginia: extra socks, gloves, warming layers, Gore-Tex, and cold-weather sleeping bags. The catch was that the individual Marine was responsible for carrying all of their own gear. Now, in addition to the normal kit of weapon, flak vest with SAPI (small arms protective insert) plates, magazines, and water, wintertime in Quantico forced us to add another thirty-five to forty pounds worth of gear into our packs.

We did not use tents. Each Marine would sleep in his or her sleeping bag which was inside a Gore-Tex shell, on top of an ISO mat (a long piece of foam which could be unrolled to provide some cushion and warmth from the frozen ground). The sleeping bag, rated for twenty-five degrees Fahrenheit, was being tested by the Northern Virginia winter. We used ponchos for some semblance of protection from overnight precipitation—especially during one week in late-January (FEX III) when we awoke covered in a layer of thick, heavy wet snow. Every morning was the dreaded ritual of moving our weary, stiff muscles and emerging from our sleeping bags into the withering cold to put on frozen boots, don wet and frozen gear, and shave with ice cold water. The cold and wet climate meant our weapons would require extra maintenance and attention. The moisture from the snow and freezing rain had to be minimized to prevent rust build-up. Moreover, the bolts of our weapons were especially prone to the damp freezing weather resulting in our blank ammunition misfeeding into the chamber. I decided the best way to protect my rifle from the elements was to sleep with it inside my sleeping bag.

After our weapons, it was imperative to keep ourselves dry to prevent the onset of hypothermia and dehydration. Staying dry was nearly impossible as our tactical movements took us over several kilometers through the snow, wearing warming layers and carrying sixty to seventy-five pounds of gear. Our undergarments became soaked with perspiration and our boots completely wet from the elements. Likewise, the last thing one wants to do when his body is freezing is to drink ice cold water.

The cold wrestled with every attempt of the mind to keep it at bay and let the body get on with its tasks. On any given day we would be physically and mentally challenged, but coupled with fatigue, hunger, and stress, the cold can make some completely and utterly shut down. At best, one loses motivation and becomes distracted by the idea of a warm meal or hot cup of coffee. At worst, he sits shivering, hunched over, his hands frozen, and stops interacting with those around him. Having lost all sense of mission and priorities, he has no concern for penalty, and perhaps, not even for the enemy. His sole focus is on being warm. The cold made the simple things difficult and the difficult nearly impossible.

One morning as we were moving out of the defense, I felt lethargic and my joints ached. I stood up too quickly, immediately felt dizzy, and had to sit back down—my head spinning. Tim saw me. "Pavs, you OK?" he asked. "We're Oscar Mike [on the move] in two minutes."

"I don't know," I said. "I feel nauseated and weak."

He asked how much water I had. I showed him my full CamelBak, but because the water in the hose had frozen overnight, nothing was coming through, and the water inside the bladder had frozen into one gigantic ice cube. "Here," he said, "take my canteen." Somehow his had not completely frozen during the night.

I guzzled it down as quickly as I could, my equilibrium returned, and my head began to clear. I carefully stood up. "Hurry up man, let's go!" Tim exclaimed. I hoisted my pack, grabbed my weapon, and began lumbering towards the rest of the squad who were already 100 meters ahead of us. Lesson learned.

During another evolution of training (Military Operations in Urban Terrain or MOUT) in the middle of a January night, when the air temperature was below freezing, we were awoken with artillery simulation rounds at 02:00 and told to get up and get outside. I had five minutes to put my boots on, grab my weapon, and make my way outside. We would be taking a handwritten test outside in the middle of a wintry night amid shouting instructors and the detonation of artillery simulation rounds. It was so cold that the ink in my pen had clotted and wouldn't write. I slowly warmed it in my hands and coaxed the ink onto the paper.

As a matter of course after every FEX, upon returning to our room exhausted, cold, and hungry, we would cue *The Spencer Davis Group.* Then we did everything we had done before we left for the field, but in reverse: we unpacked and cleaned our gear, showered, donned the coziest sweatpants and sweatshirts we had, and we ate—a lot. This usually meant stuffing ourselves with Chinese food or Papa John's pizza. On several occasions, as we sat in our room, eating as many calories as we could, slowly regaining the sensation in our extremities, we discussed that week's events.

I would often become frustrated as I replayed some of the infantile methods or games it seemed the instructors had used during our FEX. I was getting preoccupied with minutiae. Even though I knew every step of a process or every dictum, I still missed something. Tim, savvy enough to understand the overall intent, usually had the moral behind the lesson. "But Pavs," he'd say, "that wasn't the point."

"Then what was the point?" I often replied, talking with my mouth full of food, too hungry to adhere to conventions.

"To get us used to friction and to help teach us that no matter how well we plan, the enemy and unknown factors still have a vote and will still impact what we do." We were training for the fog and friction of war, not by reading about it, but by being immersed in it.

Each TBS class of approximately 300 lieutenants is separated into three tiers—top, middle, and bottom. Some lieutenants are already slated for MOSs, such as pilots or lawyers, since they previously signed contracts with the Marine Corps. The rest of the 300 lieutenants must each list an MOS preference. Every TBS class has approximately nineteen to twenty MOSs to choose from based on the needs of the Marine Corps.

The catch is that the three separate tiers play an important role in accurately distributing the intelligence quotient across the entire Marine Corps. For example, the top Marines in the first tier will usually receive their MOS of choice. Then the choice is given to those Marines at the top of the second tier. Finally, the preferences of those Marines at the top of the third tier are met. In other words, even though a Marine may be a strong performer and be graduating overall in the top tier of his or her TBS company, he or she may still end up with a less than preferred MOS. The most sought after MOS in March 2008 was Infantry (0302); the second most popular, Ground Intelligence (0203).

On the day of the MOS announcements, our SPC told us to muster in the vestibule of the building where we were billeted. As she summed up the last six months of learning, growth, and cohesion as a platoon, we were all more focused and curious about what our jobs were going to be as new lieutenants, and how we might make our mark on the fleet. We waited with nervous anticipation as she concluded her remarks.

She then began calling on us alphabetically by last name, each lieutenant replying with, "Here, ma'am." This meant I would be waiting a little while. I knew Tim wanted Infantry, I paid close attention when she called his name, "Lieutenant Kudo."

"Here ma'am," he replied. "0302." I saw a look of relief and pride wash over his face.

My fate was still unknown as the captain crept closer to my last name. "Lieutenant Pavlak."

"Here, ma'am" I replied. "0203."

A wave of surprise rolled over me. I had just been assigned one of the two most competitive MOSs in our TBS company. This meant Infantry Officer Course (IOC) and then the follow-on Ground Intelligence Officer Course (GIOC) in Virginia Beach. Given my dislike of the outdoors, however, I was unsure how to receive the news. TBS had its own challenges, but we all knew that IOC significantly upped the ante when it came to fatigue, stress, and dealing with the elements. And GIOC's training was still a mystery.

The 0203 MOS, along with the other company grade intelligence officer MOSs (human, signals, and air) was developed as part of the so-called "Van Riper Plan" in 1995. Then-MajGen Paul K. Van Riper, the Director of Intelligence, restructured the Marine Corps intelligence community in the wake of perceived tactical intelligence shortcomings in Operation DESERT STORM. Ground Intel officers were trained to be fluent in infantry tactics and how to assess the enemy's situation, center of gravity, and critical vulnerabilities. In this way, they would gain firsthand knowledge of the infantry and then have the tactical bona fides to advise a battalion or regimental commander on the enemy and how the commander might employ his combat power to effectively counter the enemy. But given the mandatory training of IOC and GIOC, it also meant these officers had the potential to command a rifle platoon, and perhaps even command a scout sniper platoon.

A week after we had been assigned our MOSs, with less than two weeks left of the TBS curriculum, those lieutenants from Fox Company who were going to pick up with Infantry Officer Course 3-08 (the third iteration of the school in the year 2008)—the Infantry officers and the Ground Intelligence officers—received a brief from the Director of Infantry Officer Course. The informal and conversational question-and-answer session was to help manage our expectations, as well as those of our wives or girlfriends,[15] who were also invited to the briefing. Major Juarez began by congratulating us on finishing TBS, but admonished that our greatest challenge still lay ahead. "If the technical and tactical proficiency of a new TBS graduate is equivalent to running," he said with a matter-of-fact tone, "then IOC will be a full-on sprint." He made it very clear that this would likely be the most demanding school in our Marine Corps career. Then he addressed the wives and girlfriends. "I hate to break this to you, but you will see these guys less than you did during TBS. It may only be once a week—probably only on Sundays, but I can't even promise you that." He then requested, "Please continue to be supportive; they'll need it more than ever during the next twelve weeks." Finally, after answering a few more administrative questions, the director gave us our first homework assignment, to be completed by the first day of the course: "One, read *Gates of Fire* by Steven Pressfield; and two, watch the movie *Cinderella Man*. That's all I have, gentlemen."

---

15   I attended IOC before female integration into combat arms.

Chapter 9

INFANTRY OFFICER COURSE 3-08

"While the magnitude of violence may vary with the object and means of war, the violent essence of war will never change. Any study of war that neglects this basic truth is misleading and incomplete."

—MCDP 1 WARFIGHTING

Some sanctuaries and holy sites around the world permanently enshrine heroes who have been born, have wrought, or have passed back into the void. Phrases over their thresholds convey the wisdom of the ancients, and some even serve as reliquaries where the remains of those whose faith could not be shaken are entombed. In the Marine Corps, however, sometimes greatness is conveyed by austerity instead of ostentatiousness. Most civilians or newcomers to Camp Barrett are unaware of the fact that a nondescript and otherwise insignificant building houses the world's premier school of infantry. Its exterior is plain, without any display of its importance to the profession of arms. The interior betrays a similar simplicity. The all-red brick building with few windows stands alone on the corner of an intersection on Camp Barrett in Quantico, Virginia. The sign in front simply reads: Infantry Officer Course. During TBS, we would walk past a lonely brick building with a quiet reverence, whispering to each other the rumors we had heard about what takes place inside its walls.

Once inside, hanging on the walls are the banners of regimental and battalion insignia from military units around the world who have sent service members to be trained there or have made the pilgrimage to Quantico, telling the story of its legacy to warfighting. One large auditorium—sterile and windowless—serves as the nave where the congregation of second lieutenants comes to learn the tenets of maneuver warfare and the heroic deeds of Marines in combat. Written above each set of double doors that flank the auditorium on the left and the right is the ancient Spartan admonition to the students of the agōgē, *Out these doors, nothing*; a reminder of the unique bond being formed among warriors within, and that what is taught here should not be shared with the outside world. Instead of religious iconography, there are pictures of Marines and stories of their heroic actions, those who have earned the Medal of Honor, and have, for all intents and purposes, achieved sainthood in the Marine Corps. A single meditation from the Athenian historian Thucydides is inscribed over the entrance: *He is best who is trained in the severest school*.

This is the church of violence.

Infantry Officer Course (IOC) was the result of the Vietnam War. Until then, the only period of instruction dedicated to training Marine officers on how to command a rifle platoon was TBS. The Marine Corps realized that due to the high casualty rates of new second lieutenants and their Marines in the jungles of Southeast Asia, a more rigorous and demanding finishing school was required. Marines required better instruction in patrolling, small-unit leadership, and mobile defenses. The Marine Corps took lessons learned directly from combat operations and incorporated them into the curriculum at IOC, including a staff of captains and majors, who had served in Vietnam, to pass their knowledge on to the new lieutenants.

Its emphasis on a short feedback loop, of unabashedly bringing combat lessons learned to its young leaders, and giving them the state-of-the-practice of tactical combat operations has made IOC the world's premier institution for infantry tactics and small-unit leadership. Moreover, the Marine Corps is an infantry-centric organization. Functionally, everything it does supports the warfighter on the ground—the infantryman. What makes the Marine Corps unique, and what has guaranteed its survival since 1953 (when Congress had begun to question its purpose and existence) is its ability to perform all warfighting functions organically.

When the Marine Corps goes to war, it organizes itself into what is called a Marine Air-Ground Task Force (MAGTF). This is composed of a Command Element, Ground Combat Element, Aviation Combat Element, and Logistics Combat Element. Likewise, MAGTFs are scalable and balanced air-ground, combined arms task forces under a single commander. The smallest composition would constitute a battalion-sized MAGTF—a Marine Expeditionary Unit (MEU)—approximately 1,900–2,100 Marines. The next largest is a Marine Expeditionary Brigade (MEB)—18,000 Marines. Finally, the MAGTF can scale all the way up to a Marine Expeditionary Force (MEF). A MEF would likely constitute an entire Marine

Division and its full complement of combined arms, totaling between 50,000–60,000 Marines. This all-in-one, scalable, organic capability is what makes the Marine Corps expeditionary. It does not rely on any external organization to conduct the full range of military operations. By design, the President of the United States can have American Marines responding to a crisis anywhere in the world within forty-eight hours.

Our class of eighty-six lieutenants was split into two platoons of forty-three Marines each. I learned that I would be in the same platoon as another lieutenant I had befriended during TBS. Since our last names were close to the end of the alphabet, we were in the same squad and even the same fire team. This was welcome news. During TBS, he had been in sixth platoon, I in fifth. Our dormitory rooms were not far from one another, and our paths regularly crossed, but it was his charismatic personality that made him more well known to me than I to him. To this day, I have never met anyone with the same charisma, optimism, confidence, and magnetic personality as Owen Wrabel. Needless to say, I was happy to learn we would be fire teammates.

Before joining the Marine Corps he had been a prison guard in Pennsylvania and embodied every bit of the raw emotion and alpha-male confidence required to intimidate even prisoners. But his dream, like so many of my peers, was to be a Marine officer—an infantry officer. And he personified those traits one would expect in an infantryman. Disinclined toward introspection, he had the kind of gregarious, magnetic personality that instantly won him friends for life.[16] Many at TBS and now IOC,

---

16   Credit for these descriptions of Owen Wrabel's personality traits belongs to Jon Krakauer. After reading his book *Into Thin Air* (London: MacMillan, 1997) and his description of Scott Fischer (61–67), I knew immediately he had described my fellow lieutenant.

including some he barely knew, considered him a bosom buddy. He was also handsome, and before the stressful demands of our physical training regimen had taken their toll, he boasted the physique of a bodybuilder. And while his brown hair, like all of ours, was now extremely short due to Marine Corps regulations, only two years earlier it had been a bleach blonde mop. Not surprisingly, among those whom he attracted were more than a few members of the opposite sex, and he never shied away from the attention.

Being fire teammates forced us—as it did everyone—to call each other's cell phones for accountability on the weekends (in our case, usually on Sunday evenings). He never answered his phone, so one would be forced to leave a message for "Smash." (The reader can search Urban Dictionary to learn what this appellation means.) Wrabel's absence of guile and almost child-like enthusiasm were contagious. He was the kind of guy who would rustle you from your sleep to stand fire watch by saying, "Pavlak—wake up. Good news, you don't have to sleep any-more." Reflecting on the saturated schedule, I am certain his companionship, storytelling, and humor during some of the worst days of IOC helped me and others find a silver lining to the otherwise grueling period of instruction.

That period of instruction would be unrelenting. As the name of TBS indicates, it teaches every officer the basic tenets of maneuver warfare. Likewise, every Marine officer is technically qualified to be a provisional rifle platoon commander. Generally, IOC was not teaching us anything we had not already learned regarding weapons employment and platoon- or company-level operations. What makes it unique as the specialty school spe-cifically for Infantry Officers and Ground Intelligence Officers is its ability to add an inordinate amount of friction, urgency, and stress into nearly all aspects of training—much more than we had ever experienced at TBS.

Friction is the force that resists all action and saps energy. It makes simple things difficult and the difficult seemingly impossible. IOC would take the basic skills we had learned at TBS but compound every situation with more and more friction, bringing a training evolution to the brink of chaos and disorder to simulate the stress, confusion, and breakdown of systems in combat.

The first kind of friction was uncertainty. A schedule, event, or evolution of training whose timeline is unknown adds a new layer of mental stress to the already physically tired individual, especially those lieutenants who appreciate being in control and having a plan. For the last nine months—from day one of OCS all the way through TBS—we had been taught to be planners. The mantra every lieutenant lives by is: *Always have a plan because the worst plan executed now is better than the best plan tomorrow.* The catch is: how does one plan if he has little frame of reference for what to expect? Thus a natural byproduct is to make the infantry officer ready (or as ready as possible) for any eventuality.

The second kind of friction was fatigue. Human beings are diurnal animals—we instinctively want to sleep at nighttime. The young to middle-aged adult requires between six and ten hours of sleep in each twenty-four-hour period. Significant sleep debt occurs at 60 percent, which means if you only get 60 percent of the required sleep you need, then sleep loss has occurred.

We were being pushed beyond our limits of sleep deprivation to help us understand its effects. Acute sleep loss does not generally affect the initial accuracy required for minimal amounts of thinking and the performance of memorized or repetitive tasks. But it does affect the acquisition of new knowledge, memory recall, and the ability to synthesize information, and it significantly impacts reaction time. We noticed one another's occasional slurred speech, slow motor skills, slow reaction time, and some extremely short tempers when even more stress was added. It gave us a glimpse at how well or poorly we might behave in real-world situations of combat. Would we still be able to call for fire, communicate to our subordinates, focus on the mission, and maintain our composure when plagued with significant sleep debt? Week after week of subjecting ourselves to toil, tedium, and suffering, we learned a little bit more about each other, and a great deal more about ourselves. IOC was primarily about enduring pain and it tested each of us beyond what we thought our limits were. The ratio of misery to pleasure was greater than anything I had ever experienced in my life.

The intent of persistent friction is, ironically, to clear the mind of distractions. Unlike routine life, where minor mistakes have little consequence and can be recouped, the profession of arms is a life where actions and decisions are deadly serious. Regardless of its placement or timing, the pervasive presence of friction forced an increase in our own effort and concentration, such that our minds might become singularly focused on the task at hand and dismiss any trivial distractions.

In order to monitor the students at a closer level, the staff captains were split among us, one captain to about ten to twelve lieutenants, as mentors for each of us to emulate and seek counsel from when needed. We also met regularly in those small groups to cultivate leadership skills, discuss real-world examples from combat, and get feedback from recent assignments and evolutions of training. IOC elevated our contributions to make us feel as if we were peers with the staff capable of contributing, discussing, and even debating openly about the purpose and wisdom of certain training evolutions and warfighting issues.

The mentor for me and nine other lieutenants personified nearly every trait of an ideal Marine; he loved to talk about leadership experiences and teach us how we might be able to do the same thing in the face of danger when the same or similar thing happened to us. He instilled in us a true devotion to being a Marine officer and leading Marines. He also helped allay the hardships the twelve-week period of instruction would place on us. However, during our very first meeting on Day 2 of IOC, he admonished us:

> Guys, this is gonna be tough and, for some of you, it may be the toughest thing you'll ever do. That's OK because that's what we wanted when we joined the Marine Corps, right? All that I and the staff ask is that every day, despite your fatigue, frustration, or hardships, you give 100 percent. Believe me, you guys gotta be all in right now, or you will not make it through IOC.

We learned quickly what his admonition meant. The long days and nights of our training constantly challenged our mental and physical toughness with classes, tactical movements, and interpersonal physical conflict—often all combined into a single event or evolution. As most people separate one day from the next not necessarily by the hour, but rather by their nightly window of sleep, our days were blurred, fuzzy, and strung together by a seemingly endless and absolutely saturated schedule of events. Day became night, and night became day; they bled together into one constant "now."

As with all of the evolutions, time had priority, which meant we were to get to our destination as quickly as possible. During one evolution in the middle of the night, I found myself running down a long road toward a landing zone (LZ) deep in the woods of Camp Barrett. As I drew nearer I began to hear what sounded like music coming from an LZ. At first, I thought I might have gone astray from my azimuth and was heading in the wrong direction. I stopped, double-checked my map and compass, and reshot the azimuth. I was not lost.

As I staggered into the LZ, it had indeed been music I had heard. A captain staff member had driven his pickup truck into the middle of the field, turned its headlights on, opened the doors, and cranked his stereo full blast. I saw the shadowy figures of some of my classmates who had arrived before me already well into their exhausting tasks for this evolution of training: a cross-fit routine in the middle of the night. The truck's headlights revealed a small cloud of fog above them, the warm perspiration of their bodies evaporating into the cool night air. The captain overseeing this station of training was blasting the track "Promontory" from the *Last of the Mohicans* soundtrack to help us dig deep and make our spirits soar.

Despite my exhausted and painful state, I cracked a smile. I knew I was doing something so few get to do. The salaries we were earning as new 2d lieutenants still in training were nowhere near what some of my lawyer friends were making. Instead, our compensation was a chance to be here—the only place in the world where we could be doing this. I wondered what my law school friends were doing at that moment, given the hour—they were probably asleep—but I did not care. I did not want to be anywhere else. This was a chance of a lifetime I never would have had if I had not failed. It was then, for the first time, in that remote LZ, in the middle of the night in Quantico, surrounded by other Marines who were just as exhausted, that I separated myself from my previous failures and forgot about my fatigue, sore muscles, and empty stomach, the blisters on my feet, and especially the scars of the Bar exam.

The officers of Infantry Officer Course 3-08. The photo was taken after our final evolution of training in Twentynine Palms, California (June 2008). (Dhruv Fotadar)

The officers and staff of Ground Intelligence Officer Course 3-08, Dam Neck, Virginia (October 2008). Ground Intelligence officers serve as staff officers and commanders in the fleet and are responsible for intelligence analysis, planning, and the tactical employment of ground surveillance and reconnaissance assets. I am in third row, fourth from right. (U.S. Marine Corps)

Chapter 10

LESSONS IN RESILIENCE

"Body and spirit I surrendered whole to harsh instructors—and received a soul."

—RUDYARD KIPLING

We conducted one field exercise at Ft. A. P. Hill, a U.S. Army base with worse terrain than Quantico. Our two platoons were given the mission to "locate, close with, and destroy" each other. The entire exercise centered on patrolling, which meant each of us would be carrying everything he would need; so it was advantageous to one's speed and overall comfort to bring as little gear as possible, but still be able to remain warm, dry, and perform good field craft. We inserted into the training area on Day 1 and invariably, like nearly every other FEX, the weather deteriorated rapidly and it began pouring rain within fifteen minutes of our insertion into the treeline. Needless to say, we had to recalibrate our motivation and enthusiasm and hope the paucity of gear each of us carried would be sufficient for the entire week.

On Day 3 of the FEX, while the other platoon was still trying to locate our position, and we theirs, the student platoon commander determined the squad who was on rest and refit would conduct a resupply of MREs and water. The IOC staff had given us the ten-digit grid coordinate where it would take place—about three kilometers. So the student squad leader informed us (who were enjoying a short cat-nap) that we would be conducting the resupply, stepping off in about thirty minutes. He also informed me that I would be responsible for getting us there. "Pavlak, how are your land nav skills?" he inquired.

"Not bad," I said, as I pulled my boots on and grabbed my weapon. "You got a map or something?" I asked.

"Uh…yeah, standby."

Five minutes later, Lt. O returned with a single sheet of paper that included only a portion of the training area and was not the normal 1:50,000—*Land Nav Special* we had been using at Camp Barrett in Quantico, so I had no idea the ratio of the map given to me. I took one glance at it and said, "You gotta be shitting me, is this all you got?"

"That's it, man, I'm sorry, just do the best you can. I trust your judgment," he replied.

"Great," I murmured under my breath as he walked away. "How the hell am I gonna do this?"

We stepped off at approximately 17:30; the mission was to last three hours. I did my best to associate the terrain I was looking at in real life with what I saw on the map. I paid close attention to the map's contour lines and whether it was reflective of the ground we were traversing in the maddeningly undulating terrain. Thankfully, we had been on patrol in this region before, so I recognized the area. After about an hour and a half of a tactical movement, I called the squad leader forward and told him we were within a hundred meters of the resupply point as I pointed to the road in the distance through the treeline. "Roger that," he said. "Nice work."

The actions at the objective were to take no longer than fifteen minutes. Lt. O radioed back to the student platoon commander to inform higher (the IOC staff) that we were in the vicinity of the resupply point. As we set into a hasty defense, we had to wait nearly thirty minutes for the seven-ton truck to arrive. Finally we heard the rumbling of an engine on the road and soon saw the truck approaching. Two sea bags were thrown out the back of it without it even stopping. The squad leader sent a fire team to the road to retrieve the sea bags of MREs—two Marines to provide security, and the other two would grab the bags. Everything had gone according to plan. Now we had to quickly return to the patrol base.

Along the way back, a staff member who had been monitoring our execution of the resupply asked to see the map I was using. "Lt. Pavlak" he said. "Yessir."

"Lemme see the map you're using."

I pulled the water-damaged, very worn, and delicate single piece of paper from the plastic zip lock bag I was carrying, being careful not to damage it any further.

"What the fuck?" he inquired. "Who gave you this?"

"The squad leader, sir," I replied.

He called the squad leader up to the front of the formation. "Is this the best you can do? This map is terrible. You gotta set your Marines up better than this; let's just hope Pavlak can get us back before it gets dark."

Using the reverse azimuth I had used to get us to the resupply point and once again paying close attention to the terrain, I was able to get us back to the patrol base as the sun was setting.

"Thanks, Pavs," the squad leader said as we crossed back through our platoon's defensive position.

"No worries, man," I said, as I sliced open my MRE.

This turned out to be yet another important distinction between law school and the Marine Corps. I was still unlearning some of the habits and expectations law school had created in me. I had taken the map and the instructions from the squad leader and had not even considered asking for help, not even for a better map. I decided I would have to get the squad to the resupply point on my own, a holdover attitude from law school—lawyers work alone. I still felt odd asking for help. But more importantly, I realized that keeping my mouth shut and not speaking up was generally bad business as a member of a squad and, by extension, the platoon. Even in this moment, I had allowed my perfectionist, lawyer, no-room-for-error attitude to convince me I would have to execute this task alone. I was lucky my land navigation skills were strong; otherwise, my selfish ego could have gotten us lost. Whether I believed it or not, we were a team.

Within forty-five minutes of returning, we learned two squads would be departing within the hour to conduct a nighttime ambush. It was to be 1st Squad and 3rd Squad, my squad. Lt. V would be going with us, while 2d Squad remained at the patrol base. Dusk was settling as Lt. V gathered us to issue his order and give us the coordinating instructions. More than four hours later, after a successful ambush, Captain H was conducting the debrief of what we did well and not so well. Just before we stepped off to return to the patrol base, he piped up and asked us rhetorically, "Who's gonna get us back? Where's Pavlak?" After this plug by the Marine staff member, the student platoon commander made me point; this time I had a pace counter with me, but what happened was another lesson in human factors.

During land navigation at night, pace counting is crucial when terrain association becomes much more difficult. However, because human beings take smaller steps at night, the pace count must be increased to 1.5 paces. For example, if the pace counter knows how many paces it should take to go approximately 1km, he must change the calculus by 1.5 paces for a nighttime movement. I knew we had to cover three terrain features before we would generally turn south, and after that, about 1.2km more, and we would be at the patrol base. The problem was that amidst the extremely slow and frustrating movement over the terrain in the darkness, through maddeningly thick vegetation, I had been unable to discern how many features we had traversed. I asked the pace counter how many paces we had gone. He told me the number, but it was too high, and I was puzzled as to how we could have traveled that many paces when it still felt too early to turn left and head south. I informed the lieutenant platoon commander of the discrepancy and that if the pace count were accurate it meant we had overshot our turn to the south. He made the decision to turn left and head south. Approximately 750 meters after we turned left was a swamp, which we could neither move through nor patrol around. We had turned south too early. While the pace counter's number was high for day navigation, it had not been high enough for night land nav. The unnerving terrain as well as the paucity of sleep over the last forty-eight hours led both to his miscounting and my forgetting to ask if he had adjusted for a nighttime pace count.

The platoon commander, knowing we were tired and that there was a risk of potentially falling into the swamp and any one of us drowning, decided we should sleep on its muddy banks for about two hours. It was now around 04:00; as soon as the sun came up we would be on the move. Our cammies were soaked with perspiration, but for now, we had to try and stay warm and take advantage of the ninety minutes of precious sleep.

The last three weeks of the curriculum took us to the deserts of California aboard Marine Corps Air Ground Combat Center, Twentynine Palms. We knew, as we boarded the planes at Washington Reagan National Airport, how close we were to graduation. Any serious mistake from here on out may result in being dropped from the class and assigned a new MOS. It was June. The desert was hot, but not as hot as it would be in July and August. Thankfully, we would complete training by that time, but still, the end of three weeks seemed impossibly far away. The first three days at Twentynine Palms we contended with sandstorms. Instructors still held their lectures outside, raising their voices to be heard over the howling wind. Everything we owned and wore was covered in a fine dust. Weapons maintenance was now more important than ever. For the next three weeks, we were pushed to the maximum in operational tempo and uncertainty. And sleep was a precious commodity no one passed up if given the chance.

The three-week exercise used a building-block approach to training. During the first module (Block One), we trained at the squad level—performing squad attacks and three live-fire ambushes, which culminated in a platoon defensive live fire. In the second module (Block Two), we had practiced enough to move on to the next level by integrating more weapons systems into more complex combat situations. Twentynine Palms gave us the latitude to train with weapon systems we could not easily employ in Quantico due to the lack of open terrain. In the deserts of California, there are huge swaths of land to take advantage of. We were finally able to appreciate the full range and reach of our organic weapon systems. The second module gave us more assets at the platoon-reinforced level, which was a scaled-down mobile assault course. Then, during the last module (Block Three), we conducted platoon-reinforced attacks on a fortified position and trench-clearing operations on Range 410a, followed by a company-minus attack on Range 400.

We had a lot of responsibility and had to conduct all the planning on our own. The staff rendered very little by way of support except in managing the overall schedule and, when need be, securing any transportation for our evolutions. We—the students—were responsible for all things tactical. Moreover, our operations had become complex enough to require different phases of operations, which likewise meant new student platoon commanders (or unit commanders) at each new phase. We rotated into various billets to give us exposure to the many aspects of leadership and support in company-level operations. We were responsible for coordinating with one another about what we needed and how we would support the Main Effort, even as it shifted to different subunits of our overall force structure. The days and nights were long, hot, and exhausting, but the training was the best in the world.

We had evolved. We would be conducting a 360-degree live-fire mechanized assault on urban terrain. Previous training evolutions had challenged us with geometries of fire, ranges of our weapons, and the location of friendlies on our left and right, which were still variables influencing this final evolution, except now we were expected to understand and manage all three variables on our own. We were responsible for every single aspect of planning. We had slowly and methodically accepted, on a piecemeal basis, responsibility for the crucial considerations of geometries of fire and other variables during the last twelve weeks; now, we were incorporating that entire body of work into one evolution.

This was something we had never done before. The student platoon commanders received their FRAG-Os, gave their platoons instructions, and began planning to complete their orders by the next morning. As they refined their plans, the rest of us started rehearsals, learning the layout before conducting dry runs. We walked through the MOUT facility to know where the best avenues of approach would be, choke points, and how the organic trinity of Assault/Support/Security would rotate, each into their respective roles throughout the evolution.

Detailed coordination was paramount. Next was to inform the tank crews as to the scheme of maneuver and when and where we expected their support. However, there was not time to conduct reconnaissance on every aspect of the mission; we would be forced to execute the plan with imperfect information—just like we would in real life. This is where the last nine months of technical knowledge would be blended with the art and creativity of the small-unit leaders. The next morning would be show time.

We geared up. There was excitement in the air about the magnitude of what we had planned and were about to execute, as well as knowing that one final evolution lay between us and graduation. At H-Hour we advanced on the first set of buildings and laid down suppressive fire on the objective before the Tank crews initiated the phase line battle drill. Just as an infantry unit would allow the awesome power of an M1-A1 to initiate fires, so did we. The KA-BOOM of the tank's 120mm main-gun echoed through the mountains; I could feel the shockwave hit my chest. My adrenaline surged. Each platoon began clearing buildings according to the platoon commander's scheme of maneuver. The three squads of each platoon were assigned either Assault, Support, or Security throughout the evolution, with the understanding that, based on conditions being set and changing tides, those three roles would rotate between the three squads as the scheme of maneuver dictated.

Likewise, we had to coordinate our avenues of approach and fields of fire with an integrated adjacent unit while we used tank-infantry integration to clear the urban facility. Maintaining both internal and cross-boundary communications, each platoon slowly and methodically cleared their section of the city. After the initial fires by the tanks at the beginning, no one knew exactly when they would fire again, and throughout the evolution, we were all startled when their main-gun rounds' immense KA-BOOM echoed throughout the city. Still, as we made our way through, everything became automatic. Our two platoons were well-oiled machines, and the intent of the last nine months of training crystallized in our execution of this company-level operation. As each one completed their final assaults into the last set of buildings, the gunfire subsided, and the tanks pushed forward just beyond the edge of the city— we no longer had to shout to hear one another. Radio chatter decreased, and there were long pauses between communications. We posted security in our designated sectors and got accountability of every Marine.

We all waited eagerly for the instructor staff to call ENDEX (end of exercise). As we caught our breaths and with sweat pouring down our faces, the word slowly made its way to each fire team leader's radio: ENDEX. ENDEX. ENDEX. We were finished! Our training was complete. Over the last three months we had become more comfortable with interpersonal violence and close quarters hand-to-hand combat. One could sense that a Sisyphean task had just been completed and that we had collectively lifted a monumental burden from one another's shoulders. We had learned: how to employ every weapon in the Marine Corps's arsenal, how to work together as one cohesive unit, and how to become comfortable and dependable in chaos.

A few days before our final evolution of training, we had voted for a lieutenant who personified the Infantryman. Every class votes on one lieutenant who day in and day out holds himself to incredibly high standards, who is more than just intellectually engaged and more than physically strong. He is the Marine who, if one were truly in a bad way, you would want fighting beside you. Given that we were already an extremely cohesive unit, this person had to stand out among the best of us, but it was not a competitive pursuit. We had done everything at our most exhausted, stressed, and frustrated moments for the last twelve weeks. After we received our final debrief from all staff present who evaluated our conducting of Range 210, our staff advisor announced the winner of the award. It was Owen Wrabel. There was a huge uproar as we all cheered and knew it could not have been anybody else. Being his fire teammate for the last three months, this was no surprise to me, and I was immensely proud of him for winning. The award was a custom-made Kimber .45 pistol.

For the first time, he was at a loss for words. Instead of his normal jovial demeanor, he stood there in front of all of us, speechless. He did not know what to say as he strung together sentences of humility and surprise. He said he was incredibly grateful for being considered and chosen among so many other great men, and we needed to take everything we had learned and do our best to apply it when we got to the fleet. "There are eighty of us," he said, "but a rifle platoon has only one officer. It's gonna be up to each of us to get our platoons to do what we just did. We all know what right looks like; it's just gonna take a lot of work." The humility of the moment really overtook him, and he truly did not know what else to say, except, "I want to thank each and every one of you for being in 3-08." With that, we took a class photo in front of the two M1-A1 tanks that had supported us the day before.

When we returned to Quantico, we broke into our small groups one last time. Captain C gave each of us an envelope with the final grades for our written assignments as well as a typed letter with his final thoughts. It read in part:

Many of the Marines that you will have the privilege of leading have looked the devil in the eyes more than most Marines throughout our Corps' storied legacy, and they have accomplished countless extraordinary feats. You will have the honor of leading heroes in every sense of the word. Don't ever forget this. You are leading America's finest and nothing short of excellence, 100% commitment, and complete love for your Marines is expected of you. Wake up every day and thank the Good Lord for blessing you with such an incredible opportunity. …

- ALWAYS, ALWAYS, ALWAYS LEAD BY EXAMPLE.
- BEING A FIGHTER/LEADER IS THE ONLY WAY.
- LEAD AT THE FRONT.
- UNDERSTAND WHAT YOUR MEN ARE FEELING BY EXPERIENCING THE SAME YOURSELF.
- ALWAYS PUT YOUR MEN BEFORE YOURSELF
- **RUTHLESSLY TRAIN YOUR BODY AND MIND!…**
- BUILD A TEAM OF WARRIORS!

Semper Fidelis

After the grueling schedule of the last twelve weeks, after doing things I never thought possible, and after pushing myself harder than I ever thought I could, I finally understood the purpose of the prior year's worth of training. Recalling memories from all the way back to sharing a hotel room as a poolee before I left Minnesota and our first week of OCS—**Marines work as a team!** There is no other way to accomplish a mission or defeat an enemy. Any selfish attitude is weeded out through the surgical application of friction and putting Marines into no-win situations, where only integrity, commitment to each other, and teamwork will meet success. In the Marine Corps, especially during combat operations, heeding selfish instincts may ultimately prove fatal for yourself and your Marines. At IOC, we learned the skills, mindset, attitudes, and ethos of what it means to lead the rifle platoons whom the entire MAGTF supports—the tip of the American spear. As officers, we were the ones who would, if need be, lead our Marines into extremely dangerous and perhaps deadly situations. The purpose of the last twelve months of training, amplified by these last twelve weeks at IOC, was to teach us to recognize those situations, plan to mitigate that risk as much as possible, and when required, have the courage as the platoon commander to be the first one into the breach.

The things I had learned and prepared for at IOC were unlike anything I had ever done in my life. Whether it was calling for fire, close air support, conducting a movement to contact, or clearing buildings, the curriculum had made us proficient in the brutal, but necessary art and science of killing. But it had done more than that. It taught us how to relate to one another in extremely difficult and stressful situations and work together as a team to overcome all of the normal instincts of human nature when they find themselves *in extremis.*

While the superficial themes of the curriculum had been "Fourth Generation Warfare," "Counter-Insurgency Operations," and how to bring to bear upon an enemy the devastating firepower of a Marine rifle platoon, company, or battalion, what we were really doing was learning how to rely on each other. The Marine Corps's ethos of camaraderie enables Marines to endure any hardship, fatigue, stress, and even fear of death, because *we endure it together.* It is the unwavering and steadfast presence of mind to know there is a Marine on your left or your right who will hold fast and be with you until the end. It is the warmth one derives from companionship, of being part of an indissoluble team. As I reflected on one of its memorable passages, I realized why our first assignment had been to read *Gates of Fire*:

> When a warrior fights not for himself, but for his brothers, when his most passionately sought goal is neither glory nor his own life's preservation, but to spend his substance for them, his comrades, not to abandon them, not to prove unworthy of them, then his heart truly has achieved contempt for death, and with that he transcends himself and his actions touch the sublime.[17]

We had learned about combat stress, mental health, the effects of sleep deprivation, communication, confidence in the face of fear, and combat leadership, but most importantly we learned about human nature. Gone was the external validation I had been seeking in law school. Our internal validations were a collective consciousness that as Marines we would always work together. Down to the individual who has the internal validation to know that he or she can rely on the Marine next to him, and he on me. To remove the structure of a fire team, squad, or platoon—or to ask an individual to endure the innumerable human factors of combat stress by himself—would very likely mean the immediate onset of demonization and even despair. What was crucial for us to understand was that no Marine will be immune to all of these stresses, nor will a Marine who is suffering from any of them be able to overcome them alone. So that when under the stress of high operational tempo, fear,

---

17 Steven Pressfield, *Gates of Fire* (London: Doubleday, 1999), 328.

and even the death of our comrades—no amount of it could come between us, our Marines, and our mission.

The night before graduation from IOC is known as "Warrior Night." It is a special night for all graduates and is celebrated in different ways by different classes. Whatever the celebration, the feeling among all graduates is one of overwhelming achievement—the pride in what we had accomplished both collectively and as individuals. And pride in knowing we had survived and made it through the most grueling evolution of training in the Marine Corps; pride in knowing that these friendships would likely last a lifetime.

Our class had the privilege of inviting retired Colonel John Ripley, USMC, as the guest of honor. On Easter morning 1972, while under intense unrelenting enemy fire, Captain Ripley dangled in a precarious and extremely vulnerable position from a bridge at Dong Ha, Viet Nam, in order to attach 500 pounds of explosives to the span. For three hours he went back and forth for materials and fastened them to the underside of the bridge in order to detonate them, thus rendering it impassable. By severely damaging the bridge, he single-handedly prevented nearly 20,000 enemy and several tanks from crossing the river that morning. His action, considered one of the greatest examples of concentration under fire in the annals of U.S. military history, earned him the Navy Cross.

During TBS and IOC we committed stories like Col. Ripley's to memory and ruminated on them as we prepared for our own combat tours, asking ourselves, "Would I be able to do something like that when the situation called for it?" Now, on the evening of June 25, 2008, this remarkable and legendary Marine was speaking to *us*, giving *us* small pieces of wisdom—what it means to be a Marine officer, a leader, a patriot, and to push oneself through extremely challenging situations.[18] As expected, our celebration continued well into the pre-dawn hours.

IOC's austere ethos does not call attention to itself or its graduates. Likewise, there was nothing glamorous about our group on the morning of June 26, 2008. Stripped of the normal pomp, circumstance, and fanfare of most military events, our graduation ceremony was, to say the least, understated—just as the building itself. After only a few hours of sleep from the night before, we were enjoying an unceremonious breakfast in Henderson Dining Hall of pancakes, eggs, bacon, and hash browns. We wore our cammies instead of our service or dress uniforms. Tables were covered with camouflage poncho-liners. We poured our coffee into canteen cups. It was an American breakfast for American Marines.

Over breakfast, we swapped stories of misery, triumph, and disaster from the last three months of our lives at this highly revered and legendary school. We were eighty Marine lieutenants basking in the reverie and undiluted machismo of being graduates of Infantry Officer Course—its camaraderie, legacy, and history. And for the rest of our lives, this day, this accomplishment, and these friendships would be a benchmark of struggle, pride, and achievement, the likes of which we would probably never experience again. I realized that IOC would most likely be, except for combat, not only the litmus test by which I might judge every other challenge in my life, but it would also be the metric by which I might measure all future achievements. And, except for commanding my own platoon,

18 My class was immensely fortunate to have hosted Col. Ripley in June 2008. Four months later, he passed away at age 69.

be the best and most reliable group of men I would ever have the privilege of counting myself among.

The Infantry Officers would go on to lead Marine rifle, weapons, mortar, or combined anti-armor platoons. The Ground Intelligence Officers, of which I was one, would go on to be intelligence officers at Marine rifle battalions or regiments. Some lucky few ground intel officers might even command Marine rifle platoons and scout sniper platoons.

Breakfast was followed by a speech from the Director of Infantry Officer Course and with a few words from the Commanding Officer of Camp Barrett, both of them alumni of IOC. We were two platoons of forty Marines each, and including our time at TBS, had been living, training, and suffering together for the last nine months. The only sense of individuality that morning was for each of us, after receiving our graduation certificate and shaking hands with the Director and the Commanding Officer, to walk a few steps to the corner of the room and recite a favorite literary quote, poem, military motto, or motivating phrase to the entire group in attendance. Each of us wanted to give IOC something unforgettable the same way it had given us something unforgettable.

I considered how far I had come since failing the Bar exam—not merely because I was doing something so far removed from the practice of law—but how much I had grown emotionally, spiritually, and intellectually with this band of men and women who had happily put their lives on the line in service to their country. I considered all the failures and decisions I had made in the previous two years that had led me to this point, a summit of sorts—the opposite of the nadir I had been at eighteen months earlier. I had been fortunate enough to seize an opportunity and knew that those setbacks had given me a chance to explore the unknown. I knew, at the very least, to be denied this experience or to somehow have it stripped away, would have left me with one looming question: *what might have been?*

I never imagined devastating failures might ultimately lead me to this place and this moment soaring with pride. I realized the difference between who I had been and who I had now become after I had subordinated my own insecurities and ego to a cause greater than myself. But this adventure, as dangerous and unknown as it might be, was preferable to the demonization and shame I had been harboring since I had failed. Things could have easily turned out differently, and I might have missed all of this, never actualizing the potential life laid in front of me. What kind of man would I have been without this experience? Would I still be floundering in Minnesota attempting to become an attorney? Possibly.

Some of us quoted movies, some music, others books, and still others epic poetry. This day was very much a rite of passage into the pantheon of warfighters and each man's brief recitation would be an elegy, of sorts, for an organization and experience that had left an indelible mark on his soul. How could I adequately summarize this moment?

As I waited for my name to be called to receive my certificate I recalled a passage I had read from *The Doctor and the Soul* by Viktor Frankl.[19] In his opening chapter, he discusses per-

---

19 Dr. Frankl is most notably recognized for his profound book *Man's Search for Meaning* (Boston: Beacon Press, 2006) (relating his experience of attempting to find meaning amid the senseless and torturous conditions of Nazi concentration camps in World War II). *The Doctor and the Soul* (New York: Vintage Books, 1986), though not his most famous, is still considered part of the canon of Western psychiatry.

sonal fulfillment. If a person is leading a meaningful life, he will be moving in the direction of what Frankl calls "value-potentialities"—the goals a man sets for himself that he strives to realize and actualize. Along the way, he may learn that his true talent lay outside his originally chosen profession or goal, but it is a talent or drive he has only felt in his heart, never actualized on his original path. Now Frankl says, a decision must be made: does he continue down the original path, full of promise, prosperity, and success? Or instead, choose the path toward excellence where a true talent might lie, albeit uncertain and unknown? The hypothetical continues to where the person still chooses the first path, the safe path, but then encounters another person later in life who, regardless of the uncertainty and uncharted nature of the second path, followed it so that he might fulfill his inner life. The first person then comes to a sad realization. I knew nothing in my life had even remotely come close to these feelings of fulfillment, purpose, and pride, and I could confidently declare:

Never become the man who one day sadly greets the man he might have been.

IOC had been a lesson in the resilience of human nature. This church of violence had saved my soul.

1st Platoon, Echo Company after conducting bi-lateral training with the Philippine Marines in Crow Valley, Central Luzon, Philippines, December 2009. (Chris Pavlak)

Chapter 11

—

2D BATTALION, 5TH MARINES

"This is the true joy in life, the being used for a purpose recognized by yourself as a mighty one; the being thoroughly worn out before you are thrown on the scrap heap; the being a force of Nature instead of a feverish selfish little clod of ailments and grievances complaining that the world will not devote itself to making you happy."

—GEORGE BERNARD SHAW

Every Marine remembers the day he checks into his unit. Checking into Division six weeks earlier was more or less a formality. Checking into a rifle battalion, however, is one of the most memorable events in a Marine's career. Once again, I was in my Service Alphas a little nervous about making a good first impression with my new commanding officer. To add a little stress, I learned 2d Battalion, 5th Marines (2/5) had just returned from deployment two months earlier and was not occupying its normal battalion headquarters and barracks at Camp San Mateo (on the far northern end of Camp Pendleton), but rather was temporarily billeted at Las Pulgas. I did not know my way around base, and I did not want to be late. I was anxious as I made my way, looking for some hint of life. It was a Friday, and I did not know what to expect. After I had found the S-2 shop, the intelligence officer led me to the battalion executive officer. I shook his hand as he said, "Welcome aboard."

"Thank you, sir," I said, with probably a little too much enthusiasm.

"Standby while I get the battalion commander," he said, and I replied, "Yes, sir."

Lt. Col. Todd Eckloff emerged from his office and walked down the hallway to meet me, a huge grin on his face as he shook my hand. "Good afternoon, sir," I said.

"Good afternoon, Lieutenant...?"

"Pavlak, sir," I replied.

"What's your first name?" he asked.

"Chris,"

"Well, come in, Chris."

We didn't go into his office, but an unoccupied room adjacent to it. Ebullient and direct, the battalion commander loved the infantry and everything about soldiering. He said he had wanted to be a Marine ever since childhood and had attended Virginia Military Institute. He loved hiking, tracking, and field craft in general. Still, there was a certain kind of warmth and nonchalance to his matter-of-fact attitude, which helped put a new lieutenant at ease. By now, I knew not to sit down until he did, and he was still standing when he said, "We might as well make it official." He opened a desk drawer and took from it a green and red braid of cord and helped weave it through the epaulet of my left shoulder.

The French Fourragere (pronounced "for-a-zhay") originated from the Duke of Alva, a Spanish general. After a unit of Flemish troops had impermissibly withdrawn from the battlefield, the Duke ordered that any further misconduct would be punished by death regardless of rank or billet. The Flemish warriors, determined to reestablish their bona fides wore—as a reminder of their disgrace—a rope in the shape of a hangman's noose around their left shoulders, at the end of which dangled a metal spike. In their next battle, they fought so gallantly that the noose and spike became a mark of distinction and honor. In 1918, Marines of the Fifth and Sixth Regiments, by their heroic deeds of valor in supporting the Allied forces in World War I at Bellau Wood in France were given the singular honor of being the only two regiments in the American Expeditionary Force to be permitted to wear the Fourragere with their Service Alphas or Dress Blue Uniform and only for the duration of their time with the regiment.

After he had woven it through my epaulet and gave me a quick pat on the shoulder, he asked me to sit down. I sat down across from him at a large desk in an otherwise empty room.

"So, where are you from?"

"Minnesota, sir," I replied.

"So what's your story; you're ground intel, aren't you?"

"Yes, sir." I began telling him about the last two years of my life. I said I had gone to law school in Minnesota and that I originally approached the Marine Corps to be an SJA, but after encountering some red tape (I didn't feel the need to embarrass myself during the first five minutes by mentioning my two Bar exam failures). "I had met some other men who were Marines; I decided I wanted to be a Marine more than I wanted to be a lawyer, sir, and since time was running out, I joined under a ground contract."

Flashing a huge grin: "That's right," he said, "because lawyers are douchebags."

The full brunt of his statement surprised me and hit me squarely in my chest. Not long before this I had been despondent and at wits' end trying to become a lawyer. Now approximately eighteen months later, as I embarked on an unknown path, I was sitting in an empty office with a Marine infantry battalion commander who had just upended that entire pursuit with his blunt comment. Catching me a little off guard with his one-word summary of my previous life's trajectory, all I could do was laugh out loud. Then came the second surprise.

He informed me that he appreciated ground intelligence officers, and if there was a chance, he wanted to give a ground intel lieutenant command of a rifle platoon. He asked if I would have a problem with being a rifle platoon commander.

"Not at all, sir."

"Good. I'm gonna put you down in Echo Company. It's gonna

take about two weeks before everything falls into place, but how about 1st Platoon?"

"OK, sir," I replied, still processing the comment about lawyers; it took a few moments to realize what had just happened. I would not be working in the S-2 shop—the usual destination for new 0203s. Instead, I would be a rifle platoon commander, something I had trained for but never actually considered a real possibility. Now it was real. Whether it was my age, my maturity, or the fact that I had failed the Bar exam, I knew I was not invincible. I understood the gravity of the situation and the responsibilities that now lay in front of me.

Knowing that Tim had already been with his battalion at Camp Lejeune, North Carolina, I called and sought some advice about how to get off to a good start as a platoon commander. I asked him what worked best for him. First, he congratulated me. "That's good shit, man. Congratulations." Even though I had all the book knowledge I needed, I asked how best to prepare myself in the shortest amount of time. "Go get the Field Manual for the Marine Rifle Squad. Learn everything you can. If you can lead one squad, you can lead three," he calmly advised. "Good luck and keep me posted." He told me he would be deploying to Iraq in a little less than two months. I gave him my best and told him to be safe.

All of the things I had studied over the last eighteen months were now hitting me in rapid succession: *Did I know how to lead? Did I know my job well enough to keep my Marines safe?* And a thousand other questions, which immediately made me feel as if I were already behind the power curve. When I hung up with Tim, the wars in Iraq and Afghanistan were no longer off on the horizon of my mind's eye. They were real and very likely my destination too. Perhaps I had just said goodbye to my good friend for the last time, or he to me. I reflected on the letter from my IOC instructor: Would I be able to do all the things the Marine Corps would ask of me? Most importantly, could I train a platoon, keep them safe, and bring them all back home?

More philosophically, however, I ruminated on the several occasions during my international law class that I had debated the strategic interests of the United States being involved in conflicts in Iraq and Afghanistan. There were heated discussions that took place in the comfort of a classroom, where everyone—liberal or conservative—had the luxury of debating public policy, diplomacy, and the *casus belli* without real consequence. As I drove south along the Pacific coast that afternoon, none of those naïve discussions mattered. What mattered was being technically and tactically proficient, being brilliant at the basics, and keeping my Marines safe. Not long ago I had been thinking, writing, and debating issues of national strategy, War Powers, and the Law of Armed Conflict. Now I would be responsible for preparing myself and my Marines to go meet that conflict.

About a week later, still part of the S-2 shop, waiting for the greenlight to report to Echo Company, I joined the battalion's intelligence officer at the Commander's Update Brief (CUB). (As far as I was concerned, I would be sitting along the perimeter of the room and keeping my mouth shut.) As we shuffled into the conference room along with the leaders of all the other shops: S-1, S-3, S-4, and S-6 as well as the rifle company commanders and weapons company commander, I read the name tapes of each of the captains who filed into the room, trying to learn faces and names. I had to do a double-take after reading one captain's name, who had already become a bit of a legend.

On March 25, 2003, as a Combined Anti-Armor Team (CAAT) platoon commander, a first lieutenant, he had been caught in an ambush near the city of Ad Diwaniyah, Iraq. The attack had already crippled two of the four vehicles of his platoon with machine-gun fire, rocket-propelled grenades (RPG), and mortar fire, killing one Marine and seriously wounding another. Forward progress of his Humvees being halted, and his own vehicle taking contact from an enemy machine-gun bunker, he ordered the driver to steer directly into the berm from where the fires originated. As soon as the Humvee slammed into the bunker, he dismounted and killed the enemy soldiers occupying it. He then made his way down a dry irrigation channel used as a trench connecting dozens more Iraqi fighting positions. One of his Marines, who was in the turret of the Humvee, aided his advance with .50 caliber suppressive fires. Two other Marines followed in trace of the lieutenant who had, by now, emptied his own weapon. He switched to his 9mm pistol and subsequently emptied that weapon too. Not losing momentum, he picked up a dead Iraqi soldier's AK-47 and continued clearing the trench. By the time he had advanced another few hundred yards, he had expended the ammunition of two enemy weapons and even employed an RPG launcher against his attackers. By the end, he had single-handedly killed over twenty Iraqi soldiers. These heroic deeds earned him the Navy Cross, the second highest award after the Medal of Honor. He had done these things before I even attended law school. Now here we were, both attending the same meeting. It was a little surreal.

At the end of the CUB, I was introduced to Captain Dave

Denial, Echo Company Commander. "Good afternoon, sir," I said as we shook hands.

"Hey, Lieutenant Pavlak, nice to meet you; good to have you on deck. We're still getting situated down in Echo so in the meantime contact 1st Lt. Malone; he's currently 1st Platoon commander and will be the company XO. He'll coordinate hand-over with you."

"Yes, sir," I said, as I took down Lt. Malone's phone number.

"And start writing your command philosophy," he said.

"Roger, sir," I replied.

I called Lt. Malone that evening and inquired about timelines. "The sooner the better," he replied. Taking over as Echo Company XO required a lot of its own work. "Now that Captain Denial is in the loop, it's up to you and me to coordinate from here on out."

John Malone was a prior enlisted infantry Marine, who loved the austere conditions of being in the field so much that he became an infantry officer. He was now a first lieutenant which meant he would serve as the company XO or be moved over to weapons company, where crew-served weapons and CAAT platoons require more experience. As the Echo Company XO, he would ensure the company was trained in accordance with Marine Corps standards and the company commander's guidance though technically he was not in command of anything, he would automatically assume the duties of the company commander in the latter's absence. We had one more phone call regarding turnover when we agreed to meet at Las Pulgas, the battalion's temporary quarters. As he fed me with as much information as possible during our turnover, I realized he was an extremely conscientious Marine. He had been blessed with the gift of being exceptionally disciplined at taking pains with nearly everything he did. He regularly jotted down notes, details, and minutiae many others would never dream of recording, and organized them with a Post-It note, bookmark, or even an Excel spreadsheet. He took very seriously the recording of accurate information. This had already served him well as an enlisted Marine, as a young infantry officer, and I was sure it would serve him well as the XO, when he needed to recall a specific conversation, event, or occurrence amid the tempo of our work-up. His no-nonsense but patient demeanor revealed a humble man who did not possess any self-interested ego, but neither was he wanting for sarcasm. It would be the beginning of a close friendship over the next two years—a Marine whose opinions and advice I sought regularly and whom I would ask to double check my plans when sleep was in short supply.

That same day I met the other lieutenant platoon commanders of Echo Company: 2d Lt. John Quail, 2d Lt. Matt Bride, and 1st Lt. John Dick. Lt. Dick, who was about a year ahead of us, had come over from Fox Company, where he had been a rifle platoon commander. He would be taking over as the Echo Company weapons platoon commander. Lieutenants Quail and Bride had been a few months behind my matriculation through TBS and IOC and had just arrived to the fleet a few months earlier.

Born and raised in Scotland until the age of fourteen, John Dick had an abrasive, sarcastic veneer that was an acquired taste among his peers. Upon first meeting him, he may very well insult you to your face, but with Dick, rarely was it personal. Over time, he revealed himself to be a competent officer with a huge fraternal heart. Despite his Scottish temper sometimes getting the best of him in certain unguarded moments, John's colorful personality became the heart and soul of Echo Company. His large personality made him a favorite among the Marines in the company, but his competence, enthusiasm for the infantry, an "I-could-give-a-fuck-about-what-you-think-of-me" attitude, and a surprising amount of patience won him friends for life.

John Quail, the second platoon commander, was a quiet, methodical, extremely conscientious Marine officer. His father had been a Marine, and he had grown up loving all things about being in the field and the infantry. He was also one of the highest performers in the physical fitness category, commanding immediate respect from his Marines and those of the rest of the company.

Matt Bride, the third platoon commander, had been born and raised in Oceanside, California, on the southern border of Camp Pendleton in San Diego County. His father had been a corpsman in the U.S. Navy and Matt had spent most of his childhood in and around Navy and Marine Corps installations. He had earned a football scholarship to Villanova and was an astonishing athlete, but being barely six feet tall unfortunately abbreviated his football career's trajectory. To his credit, Matt was almost always in a positive mood, no matter the time of day or night, how far he had hiked, or how sore his muscles might be. He rarely ever displayed a negative attitude.

We four lieutenants, along with Lt. Malone as XO, would be

working with each other, training together, seeking each other's advice, and helping one another grow as leaders and Marine officers. As we became acquainted with each other's strengths and weaknesses, we intuitively knew that collaboration, cooperation, and trust were key to conducting company-level operations. Sharing problems, perspectives, and—above all—helping one another, we cultivated that fraternal camaraderie that only comes from spending almost every day and night together either in garrison or in challenging training evolutions for about one year. I am indebted to the officers of Echo Company who helped me grow as a man and contributed to the unforgettable experience of commanding a rifle platoon.

Throughout TBS we had been constantly reminded about trusting our senior enlisted Marines by seeking their guidance and getting their buy-in. These discussions had been spawned by the inevitable realization that we lieutenants would be both the most senior ranking members of a platoon, but also the ones with the least amount of experience. Thus the enlisted men and women who were part of the training cadres in Quantico would hold innumerable sidebar discussions about leadership, trust, and mutual respect between officers and enlisted, hoping some of it might stick. There were stories about new and idealistic lieutenants who thought they were the second coming of George Patton or Chesty Puller. These officers let the gold bars on their collars go to their heads and tended to stifle any input from their own senior enlisted Marines because they wanted to be in charge.

As I listened to these tales, two things occurred to me. The first was that these naïve officers had, for some reason, adopted a "new-sheriff-in-town" attitude. They had, very soon after assuming command of their platoons, severed themselves from their Marines by allowing their ego to prohibit collaboration (the same way law students had). The enlisted Marine instructors in Quantico told us these officers sought their own solutions to the tactical problems given them. Heedless of the years of experience at their disposal, they allowed their own version of perfect to get in the way of the collective good, and they failed—some of them miserably. Senior enlisted Marines, realizing the futility of arguing with an idealistic and naïve second lieutenant, would often allow the officer to fail, in the hopes that repeated failures would eventually lead to collaboration, buy-in, and deference to those with more experience. We were admonished to not let this happen to us if we ever commanded a platoon of our own.

The second realization was that if I were ever given command, it would be short-sighted of me not to seek and follow the advice of my platoon sergeant or squad leaders. Being a few years older than most of my peers, this seemed self-evident. I had not been in combat and, besides training, had not spent one day in a leadership position—what did I know about these responsibilities? More importantly, how could I take on this new position and the heavy responsibility of preparing men for combat, keeping them safe, and ensuring their safe return home without asking for help in doing so? As I reflected on these new responsibilities, I was humbled. I thought that anyone who might be responsible for the lives and well-being of a platoon of Marines owed it to them and their families to garner as much help, advice, and guidance as possible to keep them safe—even from the very men he was leading.

Every new platoon commander remembers the day he meets

his platoon sergeant. The event is one of the most hallowed in the infantry—a mutual "sizing up" of the other. Though I was not exactly sure what to think, my maturity helped temper my expectations. The dynamic at play was a twofold appraisal. On one hand, the idealistic newly christened second lieutenant, whose recent time in Quantico has taught him what right looks like and who intends on upholding the standards of the Marine Corps, brings an ambitious agenda to the platoon. A byproduct of the new officer's education is that he or she has been exposed to some of the best Marines in the Corps— men, women, enlisted, and officers—who have demonstrated amazing leadership and character in their careers. During the ongoing conflicts in both Iraq and Afghanistan in the years leading up to 2007 and 2008, the Marine Corps was not lacking for these exceptional men and women. Likewise, upon reaching the fleet, the new lieutenant may think his Marines and staff non-commissioned officers (Staff NCOs) are as "squared away" as the Marines who taught him in Quantico. Unsurprisingly, this microcosm of exceedingly competent Marines has the converse effect of setting extremely high standards in the officer and possibly skews his or her perspective on what is really achievable as a platoon commander.

The second appraisal comes from the seasoned experience of a Marine staff non-commissioned officer (staff NCO) whose time in the fleet, especially in combat, has taught him the hard lessons of combat and the limitations of his resources and his men. The staff NCO has often found ingenious ways to successfully execute the orders of his superiors in extremely challenging and dangerous situations with scarce resources. Therefore, in the inaugural meeting, the senior staff NCO often assesses the demeanor and personality of the new lieutenant and is listening very carefully for any naïveté or exceedingly lofty goals coming from the officer's mouth. In other words, a new officer arrives with a well-intentioned agenda of high expectations, but it is the experience of the staff NCO that manages them.

And so it came to pass that in the middle of January 2009, I met my platoon sergeant Mike Webb. The rifle platoon sergeant is the highest-ranking enlisted Marine in the platoon having served about ten to twelve years in the infantry. He is capable of performing all the tasks required of the platoon commander and assumes those duties in the platoon commander's absence. His focus is generally inward, on the discipline, appearance, administration, conduct, and welfare of the platoon.

By comparison, the platoon commander is focused outwardly on future planning, tactical employment, personal and professional development of his Marines, and training them in accordance with the company commander's guidance and intent.

I met Staff Sergeant Webb in what would be my office for the next nine months, a tiny eight foot by eight foot room on the ground floor of the Echo Company barracks. An amiable, even-tempered, and exceedingly calm man, he had been in the infantry for a little over twelve years. He greeted me with a handshake saying, "Good morning, sir," as he was putting on his cammie blouse, having finished PT thirty minutes earlier.

"Hey, good morning, Staff Sergeant. Nice to meet you. What's your name?"

"Mike," he said.

"Hi, I'm Chris." I asked where he was from.

"Ohio," he replied. He then told me he had a wife and two kids, a son and a daughter. I told him I was a ground intelligence officer, to which he replied, "Yeah, I've gotten to know a few of you guys over the years."

I spoke candidly because I thought it important to allay any notions that I would be changing things or making unilateral decisions without his input. "First, let's not pretend that I've done this before. You've been doing these things for what, twelve years now?"

"Yes, sir," he proudly replied.

So in an attempt to remove any potential barriers to what would need to be a collaborative and cooperative relationship, I said, "Look, I'm gonna be straightforward with you—you and the squad leaders have been doing these things for a long time. I'm going to defer to your experience and judgment. Ultimately, I will make the decisions, but those decisions will hinge on the input, guidance, and advice I receive from you."

Webb seemed surprised that his new lieutenant was being this candid and deferential. I finally told him, "This isn't my platoon, it's not your platoon, this is *our* platoon." I believed that by giving my platoon sergeant and squad leaders "buy-in" when it came to how we would tactically employ ourselves and how we might accomplish the mission, we might work to find the best answer to each problem we encountered. I would defer to my Marines and not usurp their position or combat experience.

A few weeks later, I met my first squad leader Ian Tawney, who had just completed Squad Leaders Course and was the honor graduate of his class. Ian was from Dallas, Oregon, and had been taking industrial arts classes at a local community college, but realized he wasn't ready for university studies. One of his friends who had joined the Marine Corps would return with stories and experiences that impressed Ian, and he thought, *I could do that.* Moreover, Ian had a love of firearms, probably cultivated by his father, an Oregon State Police Officer, who raised him to respect and appreciate them in all their varieties. It was not long before Ian joined the Marines.

He had been with 2/5 for a few years and was a well-liked and well-respected infantryman across Echo Company and even the battalion. Young Marines—always impressionable by their immediate superiors—tended to look to Ian for guidance and direction, while his peers regularly sought his professional and tactical advice. Being completely in his element as a squad leader in a rifle platoon, Ian gladly dispensed it, but never failed to punctuate any conversation with the deadpan delivery of an extremely dry sarcasm. But in his interior life, he put a lot of pressure on himself to excel, to learn as much as he could about his job, and to ensure his Marines did the same. He demanded a lot from them, but never more than he demanded of himself. In a certain sense, it did not matter to Ian what he (or anyone else) had already accomplished in the past—that was yesterday, last week, or last year. He was only concerned with: *What am I doing to challenge myself today?*

As an organization, the Marine Corps believes that the best way to build trust among peers and subordinates is to share danger and hardship. The most obvious source of danger for a Marine rifle platoon would be in combat. In the meantime, it would be forged on the anvil of mutual pain and suffering. These are essential to the cohesion and functioning of a platoon, to any group of Marines. It can provide a Marine with mental clarity and inspiration, especially if command and control breaks down. Indeed, in some ways, trust could even, for a short time, supplant command and control as it both organizes and facilitates a dynamic structure for the execution of the mission in the absence of orders. Conversely, individualism, selfishness, hubris, and indifference to teamwork would result in mistrust. The relationship is a delicate one to build and maintain.

Trust can be the most difficult thing to build as a new platoon commander. Trust, I realized, extends both horizontally and vertically. It was something embedded into the dynamic of the platoon, company, and battalion, and could be easily lost if not cultivated daily. Enlisted Marines will watch an officer's every move; whatever the officer does or does not do gives tacit consent for the enlisted Marines to do the same. If the officer lies, they assume it is permissible to lie; if the officer quits, they will too.

Trust, I quickly learned, would be built on actions—not mission statements or speeches. All Marines have already bought into the ethos of the Marine Corps. They do not need to be convinced about the reasons for being a Marine. Instead, they want to see it. They want to know that their decision to join, which was based on real, tangible, and immutable things, will be personified in their leaders and peers. Honor, courage, and commitment are not empty platitudes, they are the real catalysts for being part of the organization. Enlisted Marines will watch officers carefully to learn whether those things they believe in are real and deliberate actions in the officer's day-to-day behavior. As soon as they perceive their leaders are not meeting or upholding the standards—standards they truly believe in and want to see lived out in real life—a trust deficit emerges.

Only a few of the traits I had developed in law school were congruent with developing trust among my Marines. I was surprised by the open sharing of information and passing on of knowledge during TBS, primarily because of how law students had kept such a close hold on any information, refusing to share it. Throughout all my training, and especially now, transparency and mutual learning were paramount. Instead of being suspicious of someone's ambitions, it was imperative to celebrate a Marine's success and accomplishments, even if it meant he might leave the platoon to attend a career school, join a new unit, or take a deployment as an individual augmentee. This was not a place for an isolationist approach to getting work done; any residue of ego-centricity would be sniffed out by the conscientious Marines who were looking for qualities of unselfishness, care, and trust in their leaders.

Previous instructors had suggested how to cultivate trust in our Marines. One way was to take yourself out of the equation and put the responsibilities of both timely decision-making and tactical foresight onto the shoulders of your subordinates then see how they perform. One suggestion was to occasionally fall in as one of the normal infantrymen of the platoon and allow the platoon sergeant, squad leaders, and fire team leaders opportunities to hold billets that they would not normally hold. They would make the decisions. It would give them both the perspective of holding a different billet as well as demonstrate the officer's trust in their abilities.

So after several months of working together, and as the battalion concluded a week-long FEX, about a month before deploying on the 31st Marine Expeditionary Unit, Echo Company was bivouacked on an open patch of gravel adjacent to a rifle range and training area. It was an administrative bivouac, meaning we would not have any tactical responsibilities. The only obligations were to stand fire watch. As night fell, Staff Sgt. Webb informed me that the platoon was going to practice some patrolling in an open piece of land about a quarter mile away from our current location. Given we had no tactical obligations for the evening, I said I would be joining them but would fall in with a fire team in 3rd Squad. That he and Tawney were now in charge of the platoon, and they could task others in the platoon as they saw fit.

As we stepped off, it was more than a little humorous watching the reactions of the Marines in 3rd squad to their platoon commander taking orders from the squad leader like the rest of them. I had no idea where the patrol was heading, nor did I ask. I left that to Staff Sgt. Webb and Sgt. Tawney. I knew we were getting close as I heard the 3rd squad leader's radio crackle and Webb's voice come over it instructing us to go firm (i.e., halt the advance and assume a secure posture). We tactically set-in to a patch of coastal sage scrub and rosemary, about 200 meters off a hardball road, and waited.

I could see some traffic on the road. After sitting in place for about fifteen minutes, I noticed a pair of headlights slowing down as the vehicle approached, stopping directly off of our position. Then the hazard lights came on. I could see shadowy figures of Marines from our platoon approach the vehicle. Internally I was thinking, "This isn't a normal kind of patrol; we've never dealt with civilians. Am I going to have to intervene?" The vehicle's stop was brief, maybe only two minutes, and then it drove away. I then heard Staff Sgt. Webb come over the radio and instruct all of the squads to make their way to his position.

As we approached, the talking became louder and more casual. I then heard a hiss and crack of what sounded like a can of soda being opened. Sgt. Tawney, I learned, had coordinated with his wife Ashley to deliver pizza to us on our last night in the field. He had instructed her to order ten Dominos pizzas, grab boxes of Monster energy drinks and soda from their pantry at home, and drive as close to a specific ten-digit grid coordinate as possible—which was our current location. And so, while other units in adjacent training areas were firing artillery and conducting nighttime exercises, 1st Platoon, Echo Company, relaxed in the cool Southern California night, exhausted from the battalion's FEX, and feasted on the best-tasting pizza we had ever had.

Chapter 12

THE OPPOSITE OF FEAR

"At Thermopylae on the final morning [...] Dienekes instructed his comrades to fight not in the name of such lofty concepts as patriotism, honor, duty, or glory. 'Don't even fight,' he said, 'to protect your family or your home. Fight for this alone: the man who stands at your shoulder. He is everything, and everything is contained within him.'"

—STEVEN PRESSFIELD

When the battalion was back aboard the ship and returning from the Philippines to Okinawa, Lt. Col. Eckloff told me at dinner in the Ward Room that I would be taking over the scout sniper platoon as soon as possible. Not unlike when I took over 1st Platoon, I would be coordinating turnover with the outgoing platoon commander. When I brought the news back to my fellow lieutenants and company commander in Echo Company, we were all a bit bummed, even though it is a fact of life in military service. We had been living and working together for nearly a year and the four of us had good chemistry and our personalities had found their equilibrium. Our company commander asked Lt. Col. Eckloff if it could wait a few more days until we were back in Okinawa. He yielded to our request.

The scout sniper platoon (SSP) is a rifle battalion's organic reconnaissance asset, sometimes referred to as the Surveillance and Target Acquisition (STA) Platoon. The primary mission of a Marine scout sniper is to support combat operations by delivering precision fire on certain targets from concealed positions. Each sniper has the secondary, but equally important mission of gathering information for intelligence purposes. In other words, they are the "eyes and ears" of the battalion commander, for the purposes of gathering intelligence and conducting surveillance and reconnaissance.

While I had been trained to command a sniper platoon and had been successful with 1st Platoon, I knew I was about to begin yet another challenging billet within the battalion. I did not want to get cocky. This was a billet with much less oversight. So as the platoon sergeant and I sat down, I asked him how the deployment had gone. With a hint of a sardonic tone, he said it had gone well, but to me he seemed a little disenchanted with the last six months. As I read between the lines, I gathered it was because he, like nearly every Marine, wanted to be in the fight in Iraq or Afghanistan. I was not surprised.

I asked him what the day-to-day routine was like. As he began his response, I realized I would be given enough rope to hang myself. Commanding the sniper platoon (which was located in Headquarters & Service Company at 2/5 entirely removed from all the rifle companies) meant that there was much less oversight of me and my planning than there had been when I was at 1st Platoon. I was no longer affiliated with Echo Company; these were completely different Marines in my charge with a different mission. As a rifle platoon commander, I had gotten direction from the company commander about how to employ the platoon—the scope of what was possible for me to use my own creativity in tactical decisions was actually rather narrow. Moreover, our training schedule was already written by the XO; our company-level exercises were already planned and signed-off on.

Now as a sniper platoon commander, I was in charge of developing training plans, training objectives, and reconnaissance plans, of which I was required to submit or brief to Lt. Col. Eckloff directly. In other words, the sniper platoon is considered a battalion-level asset and is in general support of whatever scheme of maneuver the battalion commander develops. A common mission is to conduct a reconnaissance mission for the battalion commander before the ground combat element assaults the objective. Thus several mutually supporting teams have determined the best locations for observing the objective and supporting each other with observation and fires. Their insertion will take place anywhere between forty-eight to ninety-six hours ahead of the battalion. During that time, the snipers will inform the situational awareness of the sniper platoon commander via satellite radio regarding the terrain, the trafficability of ingress and egress routes for friendly forces, and any activity occurring at the objective. They may also be used as forward observers in order to call for artillery fire as the battalion's advanced party and main body are maneuvering to the objective. Finally, if the battalion commander has issued sniper engagement criteria, scout snipers can prosecute high-value targets when those criteria are met. Needless to say, each sniper must have the maturity and presence of mind to maintain his composure and discipline amid extremely austere conditions.

As a sniper platoon commander, trust in the abilities of my subordinates was essential. In a deployed environment, my Marines would be outside of my immediate supervision for days at a time, making crucial tactical decisions on their own. They would engage the enemy, call for fire, call for close air support, and keep me apprised of the situation on the ground via satellite communications (SATCOM). I would then convey this information to the battalion intelligence and operations officers.

Likewise, a Marine scout sniper must be able to understand the intent of the platoon commander, execute that intent, and most importantly, accomplish the mission while operating autonomously without supervision several miles from any friendly units in potentially very dangerous situations. Their missions vary from gathering information for intelligence purposes, to the delivery of long-range precision fires against high-value targets.

Oftentimes scout snipers are inserted via helicopter in proximity to the battalion's tactical objective. From the insertion point, they will separate into their teams and patrol to pre-planned locations. In a preponderance of instances, the Marines comprising the scout sniper platoon are former fire-team leaders and sometimes even squad leaders who have come from the Marine rifle companies. Regardless of their rank or billet, scout snipers must demonstrate excellence in field craft and marksmanship, and most importantly, possess a composure and maturity that allows them to make critical decisions independently and without direct oversight. Likewise, the Marines who have held leadership billets in rifle platoons or weapons platoons have developed the savvy to make them competent snipers.

Upon returning from the 31st MEU in January 2010, the battalion would take approximately ten days of post-deployment leave, to take a break, travel, and most importantly relax at home with loved ones after a six-month absence. It was during our post-deployment safety brief that LtCol Eckloff thanked all of us for a safe and successful deployment in the Pacific, but as luck would have it, the operational needs of the Marine Corps were sending 2/5 back to Okinawa for another 31st MEU deployment approximately nine months hence. There were noticeable murmurings about this prospect by many of the Marines encircled around the commander that afternoon. In one year, we would be back on ship, back to the Pacific, away from the action of Iraq, and especially Afghanistan.

Before we deployed, I had decided I would attempt the Minnesota Bar exam a third time. Whatever downtime I had while underway on ship or while living at Okinawa, I had done my best to study. Now during our post-deployment leave, after securing an apartment in Laguna Niguel and without unpacking any furniture except my bed, I drank Red Bull and slept little as I prepared for my third attempt. I would be cramming in as much studying as I could for two weeks before flying back to Minnesota to take the February exam in 2010.

It is customary that Marine rifle battalions allow certain enlisted Marines—those who have two deployments with the unit—to move on and serve elsewhere if they wish. They are encouraged to stay longer, under the auspices of maintaining continuity and legacy knowledge. Likewise, while 2/5 was on leave, those Marines who had already served two tours with the battalion eagerly pursued alternatives so they could get to the fight.

They would not need to look far—3rd BN, 5th Marines, also

located at Camp San Mateo, whose headquarters building was only two blocks away from our battalion headquarters, would be deploying to the Helmand province in Afghanistan in late September. Unsurprisingly, given the news about our battalion's plan to return to Okinawa, there was a mass exodus of Marines from 2/5 to 3/5 who wanted to get in the fight.

The exodus affected the sniper platoon too. After we returned from post-deployment leave, my platoon sergeant, chief scout, and I began thinking about all the work we would have to do and outlined our training plans and schedules on dry erase boards in the platoon office at the Headquarters and Service (H&S) building.

On Monday morning of our second week back from leave, my chief scout came into the platoon office with five other Marines. "Hey, sir," he said, "do you have some time? Some of the guys want to talk to you."

"Sure," I said, "What's up?"

One by one, five Marines told me their desire to join 3/5; two of them were Lance Corporal Matt Smith and Lance Corporal Kevin Frame. During leave, they had talked to friends at that battalion and asked if that sniper platoon or any of the rifle platoons could use the extra support. While they were being polite and going through the proper channels—first me, their platoon commander, then the H&S company commander, and finally the battalion executive officer—they did not really need my permission. "Well, I wish I could keep your talents in this platoon, but I'm not gonna hold you guys back, and if it were me, I would want to go too."

I understood completely why they wanted to join 3/5. My chief scout was encouraging to all of us. To these five Marines, he knew what it was they were seeking, but as a seasoned sniper, he also knew the work involved in building a good, cohesive platoon and he knew the challenges we faced in 2/5. My platoon sergeant knew the same things and reiterated the chief scout's point. At the end of our meeting, I shook each one's hand, said good luck, and told them to be safe. By the end of the week, the transfer paperwork was complete, and they were out of the battalion.

Complicating things further, a four-man sniper team left our platoon to support Fox Company on a separate mission in Afghanistan. Their loss now cut our platoon almost in half. I would have to rebuild the platoon with those Marines from the rifle companies who remained. This would be a challenge. Thankfully, my platoon sergeant remained in the platoon for continuity. Our first task was to come up with a training plan that both allowed some of our Marines to attend professional schools as well as plan a sniper screener to evaluate those Marines who wanted to try out for the platoon. For the months of March and April, we would be slowly building the platoon back to its original strength or as close to it as possible.

My Bar exam results were due to be published on Thursday, April 15 (my thirty-first birthday). I was returning from a field exercise with my snipers riding in a HUMVEE in the hills of Camp Pendleton. I had texted my examinee number to my best friend who looked it up online. He relayed the message to me via text that I had failed the Bar a third time.

Sergeant Ian M. Tawney, one of the very best Marines I've ever had the privilege of serving with. His sharp mind and even sharper sarcastic wit were a rare combination. Holding himself and others to extremely high standards, he loved being a Marine and had the admiration of enlisted and officers alike. Pictured here in his Dress Blue "A" uniform, as a member of the 5th Marine Regiment, he is wearing the French Fourragere on his left shoulder (August 2009). (Ashley Tawney)

I was sitting at my desk in the sniper platoon office about a week later when Sgt. Ian Tawney knocked on the open door. "Hey, sir, how's it goin'?" as he peeked his head inside.

"Sgt. Tawney!" I exclaimed. "Get the fuck in here! Man, is it good to see you. How're ya doin?" I inquired as I walked over and shook his hand, and as he spit his tobacco—in typical Tawney fashion, he carried an empty Monster can in his hand as a spittoon, while carrying a second unopened one in a cargo pocket of his cammie trousers.

As I invited him to sit down, he pulled the unopened can from his trousers and cracked it open, taking a huge swig. He plopped down onto the couch we had in the office sitting directly across from me at the desk, a bulge of tobacco tucked into his bottom lip. "How's it goin, sir? I like your office."

I had not seen Tawney since I left 1st Platoon nearly five months earlier when we were still in Okinawa. For good or for bad, when an officer leaves a platoon or a unit, it is meant to be a clean break. If the former commander lingers and continues to show up unannounced at his old unit, it tends to confuse the enlisted Marines and usurp any bonding or relationship-building the new officer is attempting to cultivate. Once I had taken over the sniper platoon, I rarely saw anyone from Echo Company at all; not just because I was respecting the time and space of the new platoon commander attempting to build those bonds with 1st Platoon, but also because the sniper platoon office was located at the battalion's headquarters, a quarter mile away from the rifle companies. Needless to say, it was good to see Ian. I asked him how things were going. I had heard he was part of the mass exodus from the battalion to 3/5, and he confirmed this as he spit his tobacco, only muttering an "Mm... hmm." He said it was going well. He was in Lima Company, 1st Platoon. He told me that his platoon commander was a prior-enlisted Marine whose dad was also a general. Ian was getting to know him and liked his work ethic. I had not heard of him, but Tawney confirmed that Kelly was doing his best to prepare his platoon. "He's making us work hard, sir, so I appreciate that."

Ian had a cautious eagerness about him; he and the rest of his platoon had been learning more about the region they were headed to (Helmand Province in southwest Afghanistan), a notoriously dangerous region, and even in the hostile country of Afghanistan, considered the wild west. But that is why Ian—and nearly all of the Marines in the infantry—join the Marine Corps: to get in the fight.

He asked me how things were going with the sniper platoon. I explained our current challenges of rebuilding, but that I had good people around me to help make it happen. Then he told me the good news. His wife Ashley was pregnant with their first child and even his dry sarcasm could not mask his nervous excitement. I congratulated him. "When is she due?" I asked.

"January," he beamed, with a huge grin on his face. We both laughed and then were silent for about ten seconds.

"Man, that's good to hear," I said.

We chatted for about another ten minutes before he got up. "I just came by to check in on ya, sir."

"Thanks, man, I appreciate it; I'm enjoying my time up here in H&S with the snipers but I miss you guys too."

"Yeah, we had some good times, sir…well, I should be going. I'll see you later, sir."

That was the last time I saw him. But the rest of his story and that of other Marines who went to 3/5 should be told.

THE MOST DANGEROUS PLACE IN THE WORLD

The town of Sangin is located in Afghanistan's Helmand province. Situated on the northern end of the Helmand River valley, in the foothills of the Hindu Kush mountains, the town, with a population of 14,000, sits at the confluence of the Helmand and Musa Qala rivers. Straddling the Gereshk Valley to the west, the dry desert leading to Kandahar to the east, to the north the Kajaki dam, and Lashkar Gah to the south, Sangin sits at the strategic crossroads of these regions. In 2010, it was the last remaining Taliban sanctuary in Helmand where they could move freely to funnel opium, heroin, weapons, and fighters throughout the province and into adjacent Kandahar. Historically, Sangin had been called a canyon town, a valley town, and a market town on the southern banks of the Helmand River. But in the fall of 2010, after inheriting the area of operations from a unit of British Royal Marines, all that mattered to the Marines of 3rd BN, 5th Marines was that it was now called the most dangerous place in Afghanistan, and possibly, the world.

Running north-south through Sangin is Route 611, which serves as the primary line of communication between the Kajaki Dam, an important landmark, and the southern region of Helmand—barely wide enough for two-vehicle traffic. The western side of the road and its proximity to the Helmand River was known as the "green zone." Not to be confused with the green zone in Iraq, which was an entirely permissive region and was the governmental center of the Coalition Provisional Authority during and after the American-led invasion in 2003. The "green zone" of Sangin got its name from the fecundity of the Helmand River valley with rich soil, lush vegetation, fields of corn and poppy, orchards, and farms. Irrigation ditches, many of them several feet deep, required passage via footbridges.

The green zone dominated the western side of Route 611. The Marines would learn that many of these bridges were under the constant watch of Taliban observation posts (OPs) and laced with improvised explosive devices (IEDs). This allowed the enemy to exploit the terrain to their advantage and execute complex ambushes. First, the cover of the green zone allowed them to organize platoon-sized elements to maneuver on the Americans. Treelines, walls of compounds, and orchards created a natural defense-in-depth. Even more frustrating was the enemy's ability to operate in small teams and confuse the Americans by quickly moving from one firing position to another, creating the appearance of a larger, more coordinated unit. Once engaged, the Marine patrol would attempt to close with the Taliban only to encounter an IED (or several), killing or wounding the Marines and often requiring an urgent surgical medical evacuation (MEDEVAC). Likewise, the enemy would engage the now immobile Marines in what is known as the kill-zone with machine-gun fire and RPGs as they attempted to maneuver on the Taliban. The enemy would then quickly displace and slip back into the vegetation like a ghost. The "green zone" would be where a large majority of the firefights occurred.[20]

The Taliban had studied the differences between each of the American and coalition forces that had come to Helmand Province. First, they already knew the terrain, the ingress and egress routes, and most importantly where the IEDs were. Second, they had studied each American or coalition unit that came to Sangin and Helmand Province. When they encountered

---

20 For further reading on what took place in the town of Sangin with 3rd Battalion, 5th Marines (2010–2011), see *One Million Steps: A Marine Platoon at War* by Bing West (New York: Random House, 2014).

American Army or British forces, the Taliban realized an effective measure was to lace the ground with IEDs immediately surrounding the kill-zone. They learned that American Marines were different. Instead of remaining in the kill-zone of an ambush, Marines would attempt to retake the initiative and move onto the nearest cover or high ground. Likewise, the Taliban simply adjusted their tactics. They emplaced IEDs into all the places Marines were likely to move when under fire as they vacated the kill-zone, creating a nightmarish labyrinth of catastrophic injury or death with every step. Indeed, some of the most terrifying patrols were those where no shots were fired at all.

The only thing the Marines could do was to slowly, methodically, and, with sphincter-clenching stress, conduct dismounted counter-IED patrols. It meant moving from compound to compound, locating each device, neutralizing it, and moving to the next compound. Both the slow pace and the prospect of what might happen were terrible. To make matters worse, an enemy marksman was known to be in the area. This added another layer of stress to the Marines conducting these dismounted patrols who had to remain immobile while each IED was dismantled and destroyed. In other words, they couldn't move freely because of the IED threat, and they should never remain still due to the threat of the enemy marksman.

Kevin Frame and Matt Smith were augmenting the rifle platoons as assault men. Kevin's element was about 200 yards ahead of Matt's element as Kevin's team approached another compound and went to the roof to provide overwatch for the Marines responsible for clearing IEDs. As Kevin and his team were on the roof, they looked down into the compound to see a dog they could hear barking. This discovery required a moment's discussion between Kevin and his squad leader about what to do before the Marine team on the ground advanced with its own bomb-sniffing canine. In that briefest of pauses, as they stopped to decide what to do, Kevin was shot in the head, instantly falling right where he had been standing. The radio call went out: "Gunshot wound to the head. Routine. Kill number [Kevin Frame's identifying number or 'kill number']." The medical evacuation precedent of "routine" is for those killed in action or those who have minor injuries and are usually able to move under their own power. Since the transmission did not convey the precedent of "urgent," "urgent surgical," or even "priority," everyone who heard the transmission assumed, since Kevin had suffered a gunshot wound to the head, that he had been killed instantly.

Overhearing the transmission, Matt Smith's team rushed to Kevin's location. Miraculously—apart from being stunned and a little shook up—he was fine. The bullet had entered almost tangentially at the rounded back of his Kevlar helmet, hugged its inside wall tearing through foam pads Velcroed to the inside of it, and essentially went around Kevin's head in the empty space between helmet and cranium, partially exiting on the other side. The team's corpsman inspected him and found only a superficial abrasion and light bleeding on the back of his head. Matt's team found him unharmed sitting against a wall, a little dazed, and smoking a cigarette with other Marines around him monitoring his status. Unfortunately, others in Sangin were not so lucky.

On Saturday, October 16, 2010, while on foot patrol in the green zone, Sgt. Tawney's squad took contact. As he gave orders and attempted to maneuver on the enemy, he stepped on the pressure plate of an IED instantly blowing both legs off his body. The magnitude of the blast was sufficient to catapult a Marine lance corporal, who had been walking near his squad leader, into a nearby irrigation ditch, severing the Marine's right arm from his body just below the shoulder. The lance corporal remembers coming to while still submerged in the water and seeing his arm, severed from his body, floating near him. (He recognized the floating appendage as his own because of a bracelet his wife had given him around its wrist.) Ian, clinging to life, was in bad shape and losing enormous amounts of blood as the Marines in his squad tried desperately to care for him and stop the bleeding. The other injured Marine was extracted from the ditch and placed next to Ian. It seemed like an eternity waiting for the helicopter MEDEVAC to arrive. Still conscious enough to see what was happening and lying next to Tawney as the helicopter lifted off, the lance corporal looked at his friend and said, "I love you," as Ian succumbed to his wounds and died.[21]

The battalion paid a steep price for the town of Sangin. All told, twenty-five Marines were killed during that deployment. "Their bravery and courage stands with any unit in Marine Corps

---

21 A little more than three weeks later, their platoon commander, Lt. Robert Kelly, suffered the same fate as Ian and died instantly when he stepped on an IED. Kelly's family issued the following statement after learning of Robert's death: *"As I think you all know by now our Robert was killed in action protecting our country, its people, and its values from a terrible and relentless enemy, on 9 November, in Sangin, Afghanistan. He was leading his Grunts on a dismounted patrol when he was taken. They are shaken, but will recover quickly and already back at it. He went quickly and thank God he did not suffer. In combat that is as good as it gets, and we are thankful. We are a broken hearted—but proud family. He was a wonderful and precious boy living a meaningful life. He was in exactly the place he wanted to be, doing exactly what he wanted to do, surrounded by the best men on this earth—his Marines and Navy Doc."* ("Robert Michael Kelly, First Lieutenant, United States Marine Corps," Arlington National Cemetery Website, last updated February 9, 2011, http://www.arlingtoncemetery.net/rmkelly.htm.)

history—any unit."[22] All of the snipers who left the platoon to deploy with 3/5 returned home.

Ego-centricity and shadow joy breed an individualism that burdens the human soul with extreme competition and hyper-vigilant over-comparison to one's peers. This viscerally competitive environment can lay waste to the human spirit, emptying it of those delicate but essential traits of altruism and kindness. It can create fear and trepidation about one's past, present, future, and even identity. Conversely, in the Marine Corps, the group comes before the individual forming the unbreakable bonds between men. The Marine Corps brought purpose, meaning, and fulfillment to the emotional detritus and chaos that was my life in the aftermath of my repeated defeats. Most importantly, I was immersed into a microcosm of self-lessness, sacrifice, and meaning which produces heroic courage as it binds men together, proving to each individual that he is not alone, doing exactly what he wants to do, surrounded by the best men on earth. The opposite of fear, I learned, is love.

---

22 Major General Richard P. Mills, Commander U.S. and NATO Forces SW Afghanistan.

One of the last pictures of Ian Tawney taken near the town of Sangin, Helmand Province, Afghanistan possibly less than a week before he was killed in action. Several Marines from 2/5 transferred to 3/5 so they could deploy to Afghanistan. Pictured from left to right: Sgt Donald Roberts, Jr., Sgt Frank Denault, Sgt Caleb Giles, and Sgt Ian Tawney (October 2010). Roberts and Tawney had met during recruit training and had been best friends ever since. (Ashley Tawney)

PART III

A DETOUR

Chapter 13

HOLLYWOOD NIGHTS

"She stood there bright as the sun on that California coast. He was a midwestern boy on his own.

She looked at him with those soft eyes, so innocent and blue.

He knew right then he was too far from home."

—Bob Seger

My last day of active duty was April 30, 2011, coincidentally only one day before the raid conducted by Navy SEALs killed Usama Bin Laden in Pakistan. These experiences, likely to be unmatched in the civilian world, had given me amazing memories and friendships the likes of which I may never have again. Two weeks before my last day of active service, I had attended a homecoming party for John Dick. He was returning from Afghanistan, and his wife invited several people whom he had served with previously and on deployment.

One of the Marines whom she invited had gone to IOC with me in 2008, and I had not seen him since we graduated. It turns out his unit had provided adjacent support to my friend's unit while in Afghanistan. After recognizing each other and after a few questions, Jeremiah Flores and I quickly remembered we had been at IOC together. We were on the same trajectory: he said he would also be getting out at the end of April to begin a sales career. When he asked me what I was going to do, I replied that I, too, was entertaining different prospects that also involved sales. But there was another prospect that had come my way, which I was seriously considering. Some friends of mine in Los Angeles had invited me on to an e-commerce startup, and I was looking forward to moving to LA and trying my hand at being an entrepreneur. I told Jeremiah that I would be moving from Laguna Niguel to Marina Del Rey in about a month and be joining them in the startup. He and I agreed to remain in touch and check in on one another as we both went our separate ways in SoCal.

Two years earlier, when I had arrived in Southern California, Lt. Col. Bob Stephenson connected me to a Minnesota family who had also recently moved to California and was now living in Beverly Hills. So for the next two years (2009–2011), I would make the almost seventy-mile drive about once a month or six weeks or whenever we had extended liberty on the weekends and explore the city with these new friends. We would dine at swanky restaurants just off of Rodeo Drive, smoke cigars with music producers, and meet celebrities and their spouses. I had never been to Los Angeles before this, and I became starstruck. My new friends had an entrée into what I thought was an otherwise segregated world of Hollywood's "who's-who." Between 2009–2011, when I was at Echo Company just after PT on Monday mornings, I would tell them what I had done in LA that weekend and whom I had met.

I moved to Marina Del Rey in May 2011, and we doggedly worked through the end of the summer developing a business proposal. Draft after draft was completed, September became October, and October became November. What we thought was a guaranteed conversation piece, unfortunately, seemed to get very little traction when we tried to secure meetings. Then our investment banker walked away from the whole enterprise. Soon the only meetings we were getting were because of the charm and charisma of the father-son duo who were at the center of the entire thing. Nevertheless, I still thought that, bottom line, the idea was a good one and had promise if we could get in front of the right people. The problem was I was getting to be very low on money. My friends had let me move in with them in Marina Del Rey and did not charge me any rent. Given their enthusiasm and near certainty that what we had was sure to recruit serious capital—despite a lack of meetings with potential investors on our calendars—I became convinced money was just around the corner, and I decided to remain on board.

It was also around this time that friends and I developed a relationship with a specific Hollywood A-list movie star and another A-list screenwriter. The friendship blossomed mostly from the father of the "father–son" duo I was now working and living with because both gentlemen were closer in age. In a rather short time, the two became almost inseparable. They had just attended a Halloween party at the Playboy mansion, but my friend, upon feeling ill, had to leave early. So, his son and I had to retrieve his BMW at the actor's house the next day. We drove to Malibu. We did not know exactly what to expect. I assumed we would enter the gated drive and be greeted by a security guard, keys in hand. I would get the keys, and then we would both leave just as quickly as we had entered.

What actually happened was the actor answered the intercom, buzzed us in, met us in the driveway dressed in jeans and an A-shirt (a.k.a. "wife-beater") smoking a cigarette, and invited us in for coffee. We were the only ones there. We entered the kitchen where he poured us coffee and then invited us into his living room. It was all rather surreal. Growing up, I had known of this actor mostly because he had starred in and directed what I considered to be my favorite movie. Now, I was sitting in his living room having coffee.

I had only been in LA for about five months and had celebrated the new year in Liberia on deployment. Now, less than a year later, I was out of the Marine Corps, embarking on a startup in LA, and swapping stories with a Hollywood movie star over coffee in his living room. While the last several years of weekends in LA and meeting people with some celebrity prepped me for this possibility, the reality of this afternoon took everything to a new level. We visited for nearly three hours. Brad and I were both Marines and were able to tell stories about each of our respective experiences. After this—even though he had nothing to do with funding our startup, providing seed money, or even angel investing—there was, I think, a feeling of both inevitability and invincibility that we would generate momentum and our business idea would get traction soon.

My friends and I spent Thanksgiving together. I had kept in touch with Jeremiah, who was now in sales for a large portion of the southwestern United States. He made the drive from San Juan Capistrano and visited me and my friends in Hollywood. He knew what it meant to be a rifle platoon commander, and now we were hanging out in Hollywood—only a few months removed from the Marine Corps—enjoying the new adventure, seeing what life had to offer, pushing limits, and taking risks. He was a good person to have in my corner. Little did I know how much it would matter only eighteen months later.

Over time, as my money was dwindling and no seed money was arriving, a familiar sense of resentment and anger began to creep back into my soul. I had taken a risk, and while my life was not at stake, many other things were. I was not moving forward professionally. Indeed, I felt like I was sliding backward, and it had an uncanny way of making me feel as if it were undoing my accomplishments in the Marine Corps. Additionally, this added considerable stress to a relationship with a woman I was dating in Orange County. I slowly pulled away and began making excuses not to visit her, when in reality, a big part of the reason was that I could no longer spend the gas money, nor would I be able to afford to take her out. I had to do something, and what I should have done was walk away from the entire enterprise, but I was too caught up in the Hollywood mystique—thinking, hoping, praying we would get a break sometime soon. I had allowed myself to entertain the notion that hanging out with movie stars was commensurate with real progress and accomplishment. I was wrong.

One of our local haunts was the W Hotel on Hollywood Boulevard, across from the Pantages Theatre and not far from the Capitol Records tower. I met a U.S. Army veteran, R.J., who was a security guard there. Not wanting to abandon the project, but needing some kind of money, I called R.J. and asked if I might get an interview to be a security guard myself. This was the beginning of a particularly difficult and humiliating time, only a year out of the Marine Corps. I had a legal education, had been a rifle platoon commander, sniper platoon commander, and an advisor to foreign militaries. Now I swallowed my pride and went to a job interview for a job that paid $14.00/hr. I grew apart from my friends and was keeping to myself, wondering what I might do next as raising capital seemed further and further away from my associates' plans. I had less than $1,000.00 in my bank account and was surgically monitoring every cent. I had no possible way to pay for any emergency that might arise, and could not even consider chipping away at the $150,000 student loans I owed. As time went on, I knew less and less of what I was going to do. Empty promises of money being "just another three months away" became perfunctory. But my rent was due every month. Those checks bounced.

One perk of working at the W Hotel was that it served lunch and dinner for its employees free of charge in the staff break room, what we called "the green room." On several occasions, even several times a week, I would drive or walk to the W Hotel at lunchtime—then again later, before my shift began in the evening, I would be able to eat a good dinner. Thankfully, none of my coworkers were there in the middle of the day, and I was able to avoid puzzling looks and embarrassing questions.

What was, I think, the second-lowest point in my life was when I told my girlfriend I had very little money and had to monitor everything I was spending before getting my first paycheck from the W Hotel. In March 2012, I told her I would need to wait in line at a food pantry at the Church of the Blessed Sacrament (6657 Sunset Blvd, Hollywood, CA). So, in an act of astonishing kindness, she came up to LA that day and stood with me in line. There was no judgment, no shame, no belittling lectures of squandering my time and effort on an entrepreneurial dead end.

One night on a particularly slow evening at the W, I struck up a conversation with a guest at the hotel. I alluded to the fact that I had a law degree and had served in the Marine Corps. And I was now attempting to pivot away from what looked like a dead end with my friends and pursue something on my own. She came back with a rather unorthodox proposition. "What if you took the Bar exam again?" she asked.

"I don't know about that," I replied, nearly upset that she even asked.

She persisted, "What else do you have to lose? It might be a way for you to truly do California on your own."

Although I had misgivings about sitting for the Bar exam a fourth time, I thought, perhaps, I had moved past my failures and could re-engage the exam with a new attitude. After about a week of deliberation, I decided to do it. I would enroll for the fall semester in Los Angeles Community College (LACC) via the G.I. Bill and take classes in pre-law (even though I already had a bachelor's degree, even though I had already graduated from law school). I would take the requisite amount of credits to secure a basic housing allowance guaranteed by the stipulations of the post-9/11 G.I. Bill. This money would keep rent checks from bouncing and mean that perhaps I would only have to eat a free meal at the W once a week.

My plan was to enroll in pre-law courses as a re-entry into a world of "thinking like a lawyer." I would study for the California Bar Exam after class, then go work at the W in the evenings. This meant I would regularly get home at 3:00 a.m. and be awake at 7:00 a.m. to get to my first class on Mondays,

Wednesdays, and Fridays at 8:00 a.m. It would not be ideal, but it was only for six months, and I had nowhere else to go except forward. They were long days, and I was exhausted, but after sixteen months of seeming aimlessness, I felt like I was on purpose again. I balanced work, classes at the community college, and studying for the Bar exam from September 2012 until February 2013.

It was also around this same time that I decided to re-enter the Marine Corps as a reservist. When I had left active duty a little more than a year earlier, I left feeling proud of what I had accomplished but also content and fulfilled by my experiences. I left the Marine Corps because I thought it was time to move on. I had also had my fill of the life of an infantryman and was at my limit for all things having to do with going to the field. But, I needed money, and I was in no position to negotiate with life.

I found a unit in Twentynine Palms, CA. I could now drill one weekend a month which meant more cash, and I had the help of the G.I. Bill since I was enrolled in classes. I would have enough money for rent. I would attend classes in the mornings, work in the evenings, and study in the afternoons.

The California Bar has the lowest passage rate of any state in America. It also includes a third day of testing, unlike Minnesota, which only has two. And unlike Minnesota, whose state population in 2007 was small enough to have all examinees sit for the exam in one location in St. Paul, Minnesota, the California exam has multiple testing sites around the state. I secured a place for myself at the testing center in Pasadena, CA. This was coincidentally not far from a Marine Corps reserve unit where I had taken my combat fitness test. I went to the testing center the day before the exam to learn where I could park and what the in-processing for examinees would be. I was able to get some answers but was not allowed into the large room where the test would be administered.

Even though I lived in Hollywood at the time, I was not going to take any chances with terrible LA traffic, so I asked a friend who lived in Pasadena only a mile from the testing site (a co-worker from the W Hotel) if I could sleep on a spare couch the night before the first day of the exam. She agreed. I awoke not well-rested and nervous about the next three days. When I got to the testing center that morning with all of the requisite paperwork, I relinquished my cell phone, my digital watch, and any other ancillary materials except various pens, pencils, erasers, and highlighters. Once inside the main room where the test would be administered, I found my testing number at a specific table. When I took my watch off in the lobby only five minutes earlier I assumed there would be a large digital clock at the front and center of the room (as there had been at the Minnesota Bar)—there was not. I panicked. So much of the Bar exam is based on time management. It is important not to spend too much or too little time on the various portions of the exam, especially the written portions. However, with no timepiece, I would be lost. I would have no way of knowing how much time had elapsed or remained. *I might be dead in the water*, I thought.

A fellow examinee sat down next to me about twenty minutes before the exam was set to begin. He was wearing an analog watch. I leaned over and said, "Hey, man, if it's not too much trouble, would you mind taking your watch off and putting it on the table for both of us to monitor during the exam? I'll give you $50 when we get out of here today?"

He replied, "Sure, but no need to pay me."

At least for day one of the exam, I would not be stranded without any sense of time.

That night I went to a local CVS pharmacy and purchased a $12.00 analog wristwatch and then made my way to the 2d Battalion, 23rd (2/23) Marines HQ building less than a mile from the testing site. It was (I hoped) where I might be able to stay tonight and tomorrow night. However, there was some risk of my plan not working if the officer on duty (OOD) did not want to be cooperative. I would be subject to whatever his or her prerogatives might be.

It was a Tuesday night with very little activity. I spoke to the Marine on duty, showed him my military ID, and told him my plan. "Hey, Staff Sergeant, I'll keep to myself. I'll just be reviewing my notes for tomorrow's exam, and I'll leave before anyone arrives in the morning. I just need a place to crash that is close to the testing center."

"No problem, sir," he replied. "Head up to the second deck and use the office at the end of the hall that's vacant, no one should disturb you."

"Thank you," I replied.

Once again I had a night of broken sleep on the floor in an unfamiliar building, anxious about the test and most of all, the fear of oversleeping. I awoke—my neck stiff, my shoulder hurt, and not well-rested. But I did not want to encounter anyone who might ask questions about why a Marine reserve captain was sleeping in someone's office. I left before anyone arrived and went in search of coffee. The second day passed in a flurry—rinse and repeat,

Thankfully, I was able to stay at 2/23 HQ building a second night in a row. Again, I had a meager dinner and opened my notebooks for the last time, attempting to cram everything I could into my brain in preparation for the last day of the exam. But I was burned out. For the last six months, I had balanced a torturous schedule of working til 2:00 a.m., to bed by 3:00 a.m., school at 7:00 a.m., studying during afternoons, and then back to work.

Having slept poorly the last two nights in a row, I was tired. I turned out the office light around 8:30 p.m. and went to sleep. I slept better, but I still awoke early, grabbed all of my gear, got coffee, and then went to the testing site for the last time. I finished the last day of the exam and walked out of the testing site, exhausted, my brain simultaneously overstimulated yet blunted from the last seventy-two hours of being in a heightened state of recall and quick-thinking. I sat quietly alone in my car seat for several minutes, knowing that I had given the exam everything I had for the last several months. I hoped this time, with my back up against the wall, it would be enough. It was March 2013; I would not learn my fate until June. In the coming weeks, I would continue to work at the W, continue to take classes at the community college (to continue to collect the G.I. benefits), and try to determine if there might be any traction with the business plan.

In June, I learned I had failed the California Bar Exam. These emotions were different. This time, since I had never let go of them, they resided lower in my spirit, and instead, they rose like water filling a pool. I was afraid that if they rose to a certain level, it might cancel out the progress I had made in the Marine Corps. I considered momentarily whether taking the exam this fourth time had been in my spiritual best interest given its risk of undoing the significant growth that had occurred during my four years in the Marines.

Each time I failed, I felt as if I had just squandered the last four to six months. The rest of 2013 passed in a blur as I picked up the pieces again. I was living on the margins, grateful for the job at the W but feeling utterly inadequate and insignificant. There was, in fact, a double sense of loss. Not only did the last six months of working and studying not yield the results I wanted, but the last eighteen months in Los Angeles were turning out to be professionally stagnant.

In January 2014, with very few prospects in front of me, Jeremiah Flores called me to check in on how things were going. He had since moved to Florida to start his own business, and like a good friend, was checking in on me. I spoke plainly and told him all that happened. His advice was courteous but candid: "You need to get out of LA."

I agreed but told him I did not have enough money or income to get a place of my own. He said, "Then go live at my place in San Juan Capistrano. My cousin and I are co-owners of a house there; my bedroom and bathroom are vacant. It's yours if you want it, and I won't accept any payment for it either."

Two months later, when I knew I had reached my limit of rabbit holes and dead ends, I took him up on it and moved to Orange

County to find a sense of calm and begin planning my next move. I will never forget what Jeremiah did for me.

I also called John Malone, the former Echo Company executive officer whom I had served with at 2/5. He too was now a reservist and had mobilized with a unit on the east coast in Maryland and lived in Washington, DC. I asked if he might put in a good word for me with his boss, and see if there were any opportunities. I was still drilling as a reservist at the unit in California, but civilian jobs were difficult to find. I had to do something to begin earning a good salary in a short amount of time. He spoke to his command and during the spring and summer of 2014, as I organized my life in Orange County, he and I developed a plan that would take me out east in the fall.

I mobilized with Marine Forces Cyberspace Command (MARFORCYBER) in Maryland from October 2014 until August 2016. This led to my getting a civilian job at a think tank in Alexandria, Virginia. I worked as a researcher on the policies regarding the legalities and limitations of cyberspace operations. And after my mobilization with MARFORCYBER, I was accepted into a graduate program at National Intelligence University, where I earned a master's degree in Science and Technology Intelligence from 2017–2019. Once again, with my back against the wall, the Marine Corps turned out to be the foothold I needed to grow, progress, and find meaning in another uncertain time of my life.

PART IV

AS A MAN THINKETH

Chapter 14

SHATTERING THE PARADIGM

"The world breaks everyone, and afterward some are strong at the broken places."

—ERNEST HEMINGWAY

Forgiving myself for failing the Bar exam has not been easy. I joined the Marine Corps in 2007 and had moved on with my life, but having done so without taking a crucial step in my journey toward healing, very little by way of forgiveness was able to penetrate the penumbra of resentment I had been harboring. Even after joining the Marine Corps, my life was punctuated by two more Bar exam failures in 2010 and 2013. I did not confront the issue of forgiveness until I took a deployment to Afghanistan from June 2019 until March 2020. It was there that I finally began to question the validity of the narratives I had been telling myself for nearly a decade. There were two events during my deployment that cast doubt on the paradigm I had been operating in since 2006.

The conflict in Afghanistan persisted, and U.S. Marines returned to Helmand in late 2016 to prevent the capital city Lashkar Gah from completely falling into Taliban control. *Task Force Southwest* was an attempt to support and advise the Afghans in retaining control of the city and the towns within its greater vicinity. As it turned out, my deployment to Afghanistan would be nearly twenty years after Nate Fick had set foot on the ground in early 2002 and ten years after (and fewer than one hundred miles from where) Ian Tawney had been killed in 2010.

Deployments give the service member a chance to look at their life in America from a panoramic perspective, appraising what they like and dislike about it, and the time to plan for changes upon their return. By immersing themselves in an all-consuming task for seven to ten months, deployments give service members a chance to take inventory of their lives from afar and determine what changes need to be made. Many of us, it turns out, are oftentimes too close to our problems to even see them, let alone solve them. Additionally, a deployed Marine has a relatively simple life with everything they need: a job 24/7, food, and (usually) shelter. I would come to learn that it takes an exercise in austerity to realize life's abundance.

I deployed to Helmand Province, Afghanistan with the fourth rotation of *Task Force Southwest* to serve as an intelligence officer and advisor in support of the Afghan National Security Forces. We lived on a forward operating base (FOB) within an Afghan logistics center on the southern end of the city. For the last twenty years, Helmand Province has been the region, where, despite heroic efforts made by American forces, local tribespeople never truly acquiesced to the central political authority of Kabul in northern Afghanistan.

On the morning of Friday, August 2, 2019, I had been at our FOB for fifty-five days. For the first sixty days of our deployment, we had been safe from kinetic problems but had been overwhelmed by a *push-and-pull* for information from all over the area of operations and from our Afghan counterparts. It had been a sprint to learn as much about the environment as possible. We had been chasing down leads, tendrils of information, deconflicting other sources of information, and were trying to report an accurate picture of what was happening in and around Lashkar Gah without being able to conduct our own patrolling of the local vicinity.

The command operations center (COC) at the FOB maintained situational awareness through a myriad of sensors and cameras. With radios, TV screens, sensor feeds, and SIPRNET computers, it is the nerve center of any FOB, and ours at Bost was no different. Both Marines and civilian contractors stood watch 24/7 monitoring these various media for any anomalous or out-of-the-ordinary behavior. They could pan a camera or sensor around the immediate surroundings of the FOB via a joystick in the COC, giving us nearly 360-degree perspective. The fields of observation the cameras could not cover were monitored by Marines in different posts around the base. The most important one, the Ground Based Operational Surveillance System (G-BOSS), is a trailer-mounted tower with an integrated surveillance system housing multiple detection and assessment technologies in a mobile platform. The camera and surveillance system sit atop an 80- or 107-foot tower.

Just south of our FOB was a small hamlet of one-level stone or desert houses totaling nearly thirty homes. The southern perimeter of our FOB was only ten meters away from houses on the northern perimeter of the village. I was in the COC and happened to be looking at the feed from the G-BOSS being displayed on a huge flat-screen TV. Extremely cautious of IEDs in the area, we fixated on anything that looked suspicious, man-made, and out of the ordinary. I noticed that the Marine manipulating the joystick had stopped panning the camera and was intently watching an object leaning up against a wall inside the village. The object appeared to be both natural and artificial. The Marine had zoomed in the camera's telephoto lens, and we tried to determine what the object was, but after some time of zooming in and out, we were still unsuccessful. So we panned out to continue our observation to the south.

As the Marine panned out, two little girls (probably sisters) came into focus in the foreground. One looked to be about four or five years old, the other two or three. The older one was wearing a pink jumper with black leggings, the younger one, a similar outfit but purple. They were playing in the warm desert sun of the later morning. The similarly-bedraggled waifs were in need of a brush through their hair and a washcloth on their faces. Their skin was as dark as espresso. They were utterly oblivious to the world around them and that U.S. Marines, only 200 meters away, had cameras pointed at them. They ran together and played in the sand that morning. Despite the poverty surrounding them, they seemed perfectly content with one another.

These two girls, from all external perspectives, had been born into grinding poverty and a war-torn region rife with drug and weapons traffickers, government corruption, and a particularly virulent strain of Islam. Running water was a luxury, school—especially for girls—may not be a possibility (even though many strides have been made in several provinces to open schools to girls in the last several years). It seemed that I was looking at yet two more victims of the violent, turbulent, and corrupt region. Two more children who would grow up never knowing even a fraction of the opportunities and luxuries American children take for granted.

As I stared fixated on the screen, I wondered what these two little girls might hope for. This tiny and innocent duo playing together, oblivious to the specter of the regional and international maelstrom that raged on around them. I was not just a little surprised to be witnessing this small episode of innocence in such an austere and dangerous environment. Moreover, I was so tired from these first two months of the deployment, that I found reprieve in these few minutes of quiet and silence watching them—I did not want them to leave the frame of the camera.

A gentle wave of emotion came over me as I intently watched. Its genesis was fatigue and stress, but more than that, I had been harboring such resentment about myself and my life, that back in America I would have easily missed a moment like this. The resentments I had been harboring for so long had made me impervious to such scenes. It often left me dissatisfied with the world as I focused on what I lacked, instead of the abundance I never acknowledged.

Then as the older girl hurried ahead of the younger one, she turned around to see her little sister having difficulty stepping over a small mound of dirt, her little legs too short to take such a big step. So the older sister rushed back to her, grabbed her by the hand, and helped her little sister overcome the obstacle. It was an achingly poignant scene. Amid such squalor and violence, these two little girls, without any sense of the larger and extremely dangerous world around them, were in no need of expensive toys, the promise of prosperity, or even complete safety. Instead, they played together hand-in-hand, content with life by the single fact that the other is there.

For the first time in a very long time, looking at the camera feed, I saw life for what it is—no guarantees, no expectations of wealth, no taking pleasure in the shortcomings of our fellow man, no consumerism, no flashy possessions—no guarantee of safety and security. The entire artifice I had created, in which my mind and soul were dwelling, began to fall apart as I watched carefree children play. This moment was creating little fissures in my entire paradigm.

October 22, 2019, began like all the other days, and as it turned out, was one day shy of the exact halfway point of our nine-month deployment. By this time, a certain exhausting monotony had set in. We were doing the same things all day, every day, with no break and no break in sight. Our naval doctor and I remained at the table after the meeting broke and he commented on the groundhog day aspect of our deployment. "This isn't why I joined the service, sir—teaching Afghans how to tie a tourniquet and reminding Marines to stay hydrated. I joined because I thought I was going to be in a kinetic environment, saving lives." I told him I understood how the lack of activity he was experiencing could feel like drudgery, but also to be careful what he wished for and not to be romantic about combat.

To change up my own routine, I decided to partake in a trend that had swept through camp among the coffee drinkers. Some of the Marines had begun making their own homemade "bulletproof" coffee (a mixture of medium chain triglyceride oil—MCT, a dollop of butter, and black coffee). Its purposes are twofold: help the coffee drinker feel satiated to eat less, and also increase one's ability to focus. I decided to try it. But being a novice I added what turned out to be way too much MCT oil and drank it on an empty stomach.

I realized my error within fifteen minutes after drinking half of my cup of coffee. Soon I had abdominal distension and stomach cramps, and I began fighting waves of nausea. After working for five hours, at 13:45, I decided I would lie down in my room for thirty minutes to see if that would alleviate my pain. It did not. So, I decided I would try another option and go to the gym. It helped a little by taking my mind off the pain and getting a second wind in me. By now it was about 14:45, and I returned to my room to change back into my uniform and return to work.

I was sitting in a chair putting my boots on, feeling better and glad the workout had helped. As I was lacing up my boots I remembered it was one of my sister's birthdays, so I decided to send her a quick birthday message on WhatsApp. I sent the message and then scrolled through my phone.

Suddenly the loudest and closest explosion I had ever heard shook the entire building I was in and a dust cloud of rubble and dirt covered the entire space. I leapt out of my chair and paused a long beat to consider what it was that had just happened. A vehicle-borne IED? A rocket? A botched coalition HIMARS (High Mobility Artillery Rocket System) mission? I dashed out of my room and ran to the right down the catwalk. The entire building was engulfed in the cloud of dust, and I heard Marines from an unknown direction yelling for a corpsman. I rushed down the stairs and sprinted to the COC to retrieve my flak, Kevlar, and M-4 and then went to my appointed place of duty. After receiving tasking from the SECFOR Platoon, I took up a position on the southern perimeter wall of our FOB.

Dispersed approximately every thirty feet with me along the wall were other Marines. The wall we took a position on overlooked an ingress and egress chute for our tactical vehicles. On the other side of this chute was an Afghan maintenance lot with dozens of downed or dead vehicles awaiting repair. This lot was approximately 50 x 50 yards. It was the southern perimeter of that Afghan maintenance lot which was only twenty-five feet away from the northern perimeter of Bost Qalay. One of the CONEX (Container Express) boxes in this maintenance lot was on fire. When I turned around to look at the building I had just been occupying, I saw both floors of its southern-facing wall and balcony smoldering and punctured with gaping holes where rockets had impacted. It was then I saw a Marine stumbling through the debris on the second deck. Thinking he was injured, I left my position and went to where he was. The entire catwalk was smoldering and strewn with debris. Doors had been blown open, windows shattered, air conditioning units destroyed, and dust was everywhere. I began looking through each room as I made my way toward the Marine whom I had seen. No one was in these rooms and the Marine, uninjured, had been doing the same thing as I. We finished checking each room, and I returned to my position on the wall and waited for any possible follow-on attack.

We were hyper-vigilant about anything or anyone that moved in the vicinity of Bost Qalay. Common attacks against coalition forward operating bases in previous months included an initial breach of a perimeter wall or barrier followed by small tactical units who exploit the breach and wreak general havoc on the surprised defensive forces. This time, no follow-on attack occurred.

The radio I wore at all times, set to the channel all SECFOR Marines used, had come to life with chatter and transmissions from across the FOB. Marines were sending current situation reports, status reports, and most importantly, getting accountability. As we surveyed the village to our south, we saw armed men on rooftops looking in our direction and speaking to each other. All of our weapons were oriented on them as we inquired via radio and face-to-face if others were seeing what we saw and whether they could be identified as potential Afghan friendly units or enemy. After several minutes of observation, we noticed the men were not firing at us nor were they moving in a tactical manner. They seemed to be assessing the situation from where they were and pointing in our direction, indicating to each other an appraisal of what had just happened. We realized soon enough that they were locals who were allowed to carry AK-47s; some of them were part of the police force whom we had been advising for the last several months. The attack, it seemed, had come from somewhere in Bost Qalay.

Four Marines and a civilian contractor had been injured as a result of the attack and had to be evacuated by helicopter. The SECFOR platoon sergeant made his way around the FOB perimeter tasking certain Marines to be litter bearers for the injured, and I volunteered. I went to the casualty collection point and saw a calm, but urgent Navy doctor instructing and overseeing his corpsmen on treating the wounded. He made his way around each injured Marine, examined the bandages, tourniquets, and treatment he had administered, and assessed the status of each casualty. Three of the wounded had relatively minor injuries, but two others sustained severe injuries, and the Navy doctor's actions very probably saved their lives. The wishes he voiced to me earlier that morning were now coming true.

Soon the COC passed word that helicopters were seven minutes out, and we staged ourselves with the litters. When the CASEVAC (casualty evacuation) was two mins away, we picked up the litters and carried the wounded to the LZ. The helicopters touched down and we hurriedly brought each casualty to the helicopters, while the Navy doc informed the Army staff aboard of the nature and extent of their injuries and the care he had rendered. This was nearly impossible to do over the noise of the rotors. Within four minutes, the casualties were loaded and secure, and the helicopters lifted off, leaving the smoldering FOB in an eerie quiet. We maintained 100 percent security for the next several hours.

We learned in the immediate aftermath of the attack that more than a dozen rockets had been launched in a single direct volley against our FOB from a compound in Bost Qalay. The perpetrators of the attack had snuck rockets into the village via car or truck, but only two or three at a time. Then they had disguised the fruits of their labor by integrating the rockets into the literal bricks and mortar of a compound. Individual rockets were set into deliberately made spaces and gaps in the wall of the compound. Thus, when observed from our FOB nothing seemed suspicious. The timing device had likely been an archaic contraption of circuitous metal wires charged with electrical current. The live terminals were separated by floating them on the surface of the water in a bucket. Puncturing the bucket meant water slowly drained out, bringing the live terminals closer and closer together, which in turn connected to the firing device. Thus, with the rockets in place, after the perpetrators punctured the hole, they had approximately fifteen minutes to depart the scene before the water drained out, the terminals met, and the rockets fired.

I had been approximately thirty feet away from where the rockets impacted as I tied my boots and sent my sister a birthday text. As I reflected on that day's events and how close I came to being seriously injured or killed, I was once again forced to challenge the paradigm I had been living within. I had seen crippling poverty, brutal tribal violence, rampant corruption, and a community teetering on the brink of economic collapse. Having a brush with death forced me to reconsider the self-contempt, shame, and resentment I had been harboring for several years. The status quo of Helmand Province, and most especially the rocket attack, gave me a crucial perspective about my failure, and more importantly, how bankrupt the illogical regressions and "dot-connecting" that had been occurring in my mind actually were.

It was during deployment I realized I had been holding myself hostage to resentment and anger about life, despite my achievements. I had conceded the agency of my happiness and my own spiritual well-being to fate or certain powers that threatened to rob me of my very self. Before Afghanistan, I thought myself unworthy of happiness, and I did not take spiritual accomplishments or progress seriously. I had placed my happiness in external events and had adopted the notion that I was unworthy of it.

Where schadenfreude is rooted in envy and hating to see other men happy, resentment is a particularly sinister form of self-destruction that casts a different kind of shadow over a life, robbing it of delight, joy, and peace. It keeps the comfort just out of reach and can make even love impossible. Resentment is the single greatest factor that can affect a person who has failed. It keeps its victims in a bondage of spite, virulence, and anger. Rooted in self-contempt and amplified by shame, resentment ultimately says: *I am not worthy of happiness.* It was not until I returned from Afghanistan that I realized the resentment I harbored had blinded me from perceiving the realm of the unknown as a potential for growth, adventure, and value.

Law school was an environment built on external validation. Grades were not merely evaluative, but instead were the barometer for how the legal industry identifies you, stratifies you, and compares you to other law students and future attorneys. Law school scrutinizes nearly every academic aspect about its students: GPA, class rank, writing ability, and prospects for employment, and it is ruthless in those stratifications. It engenders a state of mind conditioned by exposure to an environment where it was not only *every-man-or-woman-for-themselves*, but also, *what-does-every-person's-opinion-make-me-think-of-myself?* Failing the Bar exam (or anything one has diligently striven for) is not receiving external validation and being forced to stand outside the group he has tried to be a part of. Failure is an anomaly not initially recognized and represents an entirely unknown world; exposure to it generates fear, inadequacy, and worst of all, shame and resentment.

As time went on, the mindset I adopted manufactured a certain view of reality, such that my previous failure became the common denominator of all my present-day problems, both big and small. Even several years after these setbacks and ostensibly "moving on," whenever I encountered a problem or made a mistake, the resentment I harbored illogically sent my mind retreating to what I considered the genesis of all of it—failure. My mind would string together causal relationships in reverse chronological order, telling myself the reason for the current mistake or error was caused by the circumstances I was in, which were caused by previous circumstances, which in turn found their root cause in failing the Bar. Soon the singular event of my past cast a dark shadow over my present and even future undertakings. This is the true danger of resentment. I illogically connected my present state to an isolated event in the past and, as a result, the menacing sense of failure and all its insecurities hijacked my life. I had falsely connected any current negative experience inexorably to failing the Bar exam, thereby never truly liberating myself from its paralyzing grip and bondage of myself. And it takes a great effort to see what is under one's nose.

The Marine Corps and the experiences I have derived from it challenged my long-held beliefs. I have experienced events and people I would have never encountered had I not failed the Bar exam four times and been confronted by life's questions. My old paradigm compared my current self to an imaginary self. My avatar had passed the Bar exam, was a seasoned attorney, and was on his way to becoming a partner at a law firm in New York City or San Francisco. This fictional character was living a charmed life inside my head. No matter what I might accomplish in real life, my avatar would do me one better and dwarf whatever real-world achievement I might attain. I was comparing facts to fiction, and fiction always read as a better story in my mind's eye. I realized, however, the narrative I told myself—the narrative in which I had created an avatar—was one of success. I was comparing my real life to my imagined life within a success narrative.

When we speak about success, we balance it against failure. The success narrative is both retrospective and external in its focus. It asks, *How well did I do compared to what someone else did before?* This is a twofold problem. First, it looks at life in retrospect and scrutinizes things that cannot be changed. Second, it compares the body of my work to that of someone else's work (including if that someone else is my own avatar).

The success narrative is the other side of schadenfreude. It focuses outward on the achievements of others relative to one's own achievements, but without any understanding or intuition of that person's agency, circumstance, or personal struggles and setbacks. In short, in a success narrative, we know nothing about the lives of those whom we compare ourselves to, but insist on looking at the world through the binary "either/or" proposition of success or failure compared to their achievements. Throughout law school and through the tumultuous time of my exam failures, viewing life within a success narrative resulted in *life shaping me* and pushing back in the form external validation, creating insecurities, selfishness, incessant comparison of myself to others, and identifying only with status and material gain. It was at the cost of fulfillment and purpose.

The experiences I had in both Los Angeles and Afghanistan would help me gain perspective about the world and where I derived my own sense of value and meaning. I realized this narrative of success had not served me well because I could never escape the specter of it. And worse, that blind pursuit of success in a chosen profession had become detrimental to my development as a man. Comparing myself externally to my avatar, or even others who were living a life I thought I wanted, undermined any good or amazing achievement I might actually accomplish. Or conversely, it would direct my mind to an illogical "but for" conclusion: *If I hadn't failed the Bar exam, my life would be amazing.* This latter narrative was particularly sinister because I found myself competing against an avatar and neutralized any goodness I might truly create for myself in my actual life. Upon returning from deployment, I considered why my growth had been stifled and how I might take myself out of this bankrupt binary proposition of life.

Since coming to these realizations I have tried to live out a narrative of excellence. This narrative, unlike its counterpart, looks inward and forward. It asks, *How well am I doing compared to my own potential?* By looking inwardly at my own capability, trials, and achievements, I could appraise how much I have accomplished, compared to what I have gone through and what I might still achieve. The excellence narrative forces one to appraise where he is in life relative to his capacity, accounting for his setbacks, skills, talents, and opportunities. With an inward and forward perspective, the excellence narrative responds to life's questions in the affirmative—seeking to live up to one's potential despite setbacks, instead of assuming life's setbacks are permanent and irrevocable.

The excellence narrative implies that one is the active agent who has fired at a target, and even once fired, he might still revector himself on the way to his target. The excellence narrative makes allowances for "in-stride" adjustments accounting for day-to-day activities and an honest appraisal of one's actions and achievements compared to one's current state and potential—it is not binary. Real life is more complicated than the success narrative allows. There is always a sense of becoming—of actualizing potential—the excellence narrative allows one to move along a spectrum or continuum instead of placing oneself into one category or another.

The process of shifting one's mindset from the success narrative to the excellence narrative means transferring emphasis from the external to the internal world—from the macro to the micro; a retreat from the desperations of the wasteland of external validation from others, of the peace of being secure with who you are. When I returned from deployment, after seeing the current state of affairs in Helmand Province and coming uncomfortably close with the prospect of being killed, I realized that I had lived a life more meaningful than my avatar ever could; likewise, the entire notion of him in my mind's eye began to crumble and fall apart. Not only was I able to stop comparing myself to the lives of others, but I was also finally able to cease comparing my life to the superlative avatar I had created out of insecurity, the pursuit of money, and the desire for status. For the first time, my ideal self was *my self.*

CONCLUSION

"There is only one thing I fear, not to be worthy of my sufferings."

—FYODOR DOSTOYEVSKY

What my soul sought was made manifest in my failure, and I very likely would have never realized it had I not failed the Bar exam. I had to consider how—if at all—this failure might be ennobling. To repress this experience and not adapt to my new reality of life would likely mean continual existence in the wasteland of the success narrative. And it would restrict me from finding meaning, or worse, lead me to more harmful coping mechanisms and behaviors. It has been imperative for me not to succumb to resentment. After my failures, I did not know where I was in life or where I was going. No matter how badly or dynamically I wanted to shape my life by pursuing a career of being an attorney, I lacked a true sense of purpose and felt incomplete.

I had neglected to guard myself against envy, avarice, selfishness, and insecurity. I almost completely accepted the false premise that failure was my lot in life and that I would be unworthy of happiness. My spirit had not been healthy enough to cope with the effects of failure. If I was going to stop the downward spiral and somehow reshape my life, I would need to forgive myself. After the financial and temporal investment of law school, I thought there was no way to change course in pursuit of a life I thought I wanted, driven completely by my own shortsightedness and fixation on financial ascendancy. Unsurprisingly, given the superficiality of those goals, failure was extremely difficult to endure.

The qualitative distinction life had foisted upon me meant I needed to strive for something better, at least better than who I used to be. I will not naïvely tell someone that they should accept who they are; that they are and will be OK. I was in the group that had failed, and I was not OK. I was bitterly unhappy with myself and the world. All I knew was that I had to pivot and change direction. Only in retrospect did I come to realize that in my failures lay opportunity. Once I realized it, my entire view of the world changed. It was the epiphany that the very thing preventing me from achieving or pursuing a goal had something to teach me that took me to a place that forced me to pursue a higher ideal.

Here was a chance to change my attitude so I could realize certain value potentialities—the world as it is versus the world as it could be. The devastating experience of failing the Bar exam was, in fact, the value potential to transform who I was. In other words, if my negativity was a function of my failure and lack of station in life, becoming a Marine officer was a function of the value potentialities presented to me by the questions life was posing. Attitudinal values of my situation helped me choose a course of reshaping my life and respond to the restraints upon my being an attorney. They provided me with a new world of values. I had to ask myself this question: *How had the world presented itself, and how should I act in it?* I still had the means to decide how I would approach the future—would I wallow in my isolated defeatist existence, or would I have the attitude to realize I could shape my life again?

Even though one's encounter with chaos may be involuntary and unwanted, it is an opportunity—an opportunity to willfully and courageously confront it and creatively explore the unknown. Only by transforming one's interior life will you begin the process of mining the experience for some kind of significance so that you might be able to draw meaning from it, and hopefully, by doing so, be an example and help others find meaning in their own suffering. During OCS, if concerned solely with what the drill instructors or staff think of him, the officer candidate will fail. Likewise, he will also fail in the fleet, or worse, get himself or his Marines killed, if concerned only about himself or what his Marines think of him. He must embody those principles which the Marine Corps upholds, those principles which demand the very best. Though your men may grumble for enforcing the standard, they will only see you as weak if you do not. The interior life of a Marine officer means enforcing the standards even when you are unpopular. Internal validation meant I needed to adapt certain standards for myself, and only myself. This is why OCS is a screening and evaluation process. A commission was mine to lose, and I would lose it if I thought of merely following the rules, answering what I thought instructors wanted, and treating it like I had most of my education up to that point—*external validation from the institution.* It was incumbent upon me to develop the inner character traits of the man I wanted to be.

The individual seeking external validation asks himself, *Am I who you want me to be?* The unique characteristic of the Marine Corps is that the service's identity is personified in the individual. It is the only branch of service where the title of the organization is the same title given to each person. Each is called "Marine," and therefore identifies himself as one. Being a Marine is not simply something one has done or passively undergone. It is something one *is*. Every Marine attempts to personify those traits that the archetypal Marine represents. Being motivated by external validation to be called Marine, just as external validation to be called lawyer, does not guarantee success in earning a commission; one must adopt individual traits.

Only after an internal transformation, and likewise validation of truly personifying those traits, will he be considered part of the group. Until then, he is outside the group and no amount of desire, checking-the-boxes, or superficialities will gain him admittance. Everyone must constantly ask, *Am I upholding the principles and embodying the traits of the ideal?* Internal validation comes from how well one measures up to the standards one holds for oneself; measuring oneself against those things held at the spiritual, emotional, and intellectual core. They cannot be taken away or removed by the institution. They are held forever because *he or she* has adopted these traits as a part of his or her own character. Internal validation asks, *Am I who I want to be?*

I want to bear my sufferings and failures as genuine inner achievements. It was the spiritual freedom to actualize potential and create something out of nothing that helped me find meaning in my failures and setbacks. In response to the question life posed to me, I had a chance to actualize or forgo the opportunities of achieving the moral values that an unexpected, unwanted, and difficult situation had afforded me. The choices we make from our consciousness shape the very fabric of reality. To take something out of its potential state and actualize it brings something very specific into the universe. That thing—big or small—will now affect you and will affect the consciousness of others who encounter it. This, in turn, may make them choose something and take that thing out of potentiality. As I have reflected on the hurdles I overcame and the hardships I endured, I must now ask myself, *Am I worthy of my sufferings?*

I had to consider that taking a different path may open myself up to the possibility of advancement, by letting go of the life I had planned in order to live the life that was waiting for me.[23] The only way I would find purpose would be by dissolving my ego into a task of service. Only in retrospect have I realized that serving my country and reducing myself to a single number among the general population of thousands allowed me to find a life of meaning and purpose. By eschewing a life I thought I wanted and living, instead, a life where my true talents might lie—as an officer in the United States Marine Corps—my inner fulfillment would come from accomplishing what I *and only I* could do. I placed my personal identity behind the title *U.S. Marine* and became part of a movement, a cause, a Corps.

Failure often brings with it suffering, and suffering has to mean something. In order to find that meaning, I would need to respond to life's question. Life was asking *me* whether there were values to be actualized—even in my failure. Responding to this question would require me to actualize values—creative,

---

23 Joseph Campbell, *The Hero with a Thousand Faces* (New York: Pantheon Books, 1953), 97–109.

experiential, and attitudinal. Had I not failed the Bar exam, I may not have joined the Marine Corps and ended up leading Marines; nor would I have ended up in Southern California and left active service to join an e-commerce startup. And if I had not become versed in the importance of data and networks, it is likely I would not have been chosen to mobilize at MARFORCYBER, which led to a master's degree, working at a think tank, deploying to Afghanistan, and now work as a consultant in artificial intelligence ethics, governance, and regulation. I can only connect the dots looking backwards.

The question life was posing to me was, *How do I conceptualize myself as one who can confront chaos and overcome failure?* My inability to answer this question meant I risked remaining full of insecurities and self-doubt, and fear of the unknown. Shirking my responsibility to respond to this question would prohibit me from finding the meaning of my failure. If I refused to respond, then I would always be plagued by the question of *whether I am worthy of my sufferings.* My internal validation meant I had to forge meaning on the anvil of suffering. The irony was that I had been conditioned and comfortable in an environment where external validation was my *raison d'être,* which only made me more selfish and insecure. External validation developed in me the trait opposite of altruism. Only by becoming part of something greater than myself did I realize I might become my ideal self.

I had to decide whether I would allow my future to yield to my past, to yield to suffering. Instead, only I would be able to confront the chaos. Only I could answer life's question. I was compelled to explore the unknown and move in what I thought was a positive direction. I believe it was not unfortunate that it happened; it is fortunate that it happened to *me*. I had to confront the chaos of suffering that might destroy me and engage in something meaningful enough to justify the suffering. I could only respond to the question of life by answering *for* my life.

Every good thing in my life that has happened to me since I joined the Marine Corps was because I joined the Marine Corps. I understood my sufferings and failures might redeem themselves by telling the truth of what I have experienced. My aspiration is that I can help at least one person who may feel desperate after suffering a significant setback or failure, or a series of them, and show that it is possible to still find meaning and purpose. Never could I have imagined that my failures might open up such a world of opportunities and paths for me. But we know little of our true potential—and in that ignorance lies our hope.

AUTHOR'S NOTE AND ACKNOWLEDGMENTS

This book began as a short piece I wrote about how important my graduation from Infantry Officer Course was for me. I cannot even remember why I began writing in the first place. I never really intended on publishing it and considered abandoning it altogether after my backpack containing my computer and all files on it was stolen in Italy. Friends encouraged me to keep writing—sensing perhaps there was more to the story and that it might be worth telling. As I persisted, I realized I might share my struggles about failure, repeated devastating setbacks, and starting-over with those who might find themselves in a similar situation. And most importantly, writing forced me to take inventory of my life and acknowledge that the U.S. Marine Corps lay at the center of my resilience and any sense of accomplishment and meaning in it. Draft after draft, and through the (patient) reassurance of my friends that I had embarked on something meaningful, a narrative of resilience, transcendence, and hope emerged. All events are portrayed honestly and are, to the best of my knowledge, historically accurate.

For further reading about law school and the legal profession, I recommend Scott Turow's *One L*, John Jay Osborn's *The Paper Chase*, Brian Tannebaum's *The Practice*, Paul Campos's *Don't Go to Law School (Unless)*, Brian Cuban's *The Addicted Lawyer*, Anthony Kronman's *The Lost Lawyer*, and Stephen Snyder's *Stress Reduction for Lawyers, Law Students, and Legal Professionals*.

For further reading about the Marines and the warrior ethos, I recommend Steven Pressfield's *Gates of Fire*, E. B. Sledge's *With the Old Breed*, Thomas Ricks's *Making the Corps*, Mark Treanor's *A Quiet Cadence*, Charles U. Daly's *Make Peace or Die*, James Webb's *Fields of Fire*, Tom Schueman's *Always Faithful*, Karl Marlantes's *Matterhorn*, Nate Fick's *One Bullet Away*, William Manchester's *Goodbye Darkness*, and Sebastian Junger's *Tribe* and *War*.

I thank my parents Reginald and Kathy, my sisters Kelly, Erin, Sara, Katie, Megan, Molly, and Mary, and my brother Mark.

The officers and staff of Infantry Officer Course 3-08.

My fellow platoon commanders John Quail, Matt Bride, John Dick, and John Malone (Executive Officer): you are brothers in the truest sense. My company commanders David Denial and David Wright. To Michael Webb who put out more fires than I will ever know. Thank you to Ronny Montez who helped shape my perspective of being a battalionlevel asset. Todd Eckloff who gave this ground intel officer an opportunity to command a rifle platoon and a scout sniper platoon. They will be the best job and coolest job I ever have.

I am forever grateful to the Marines and Corpsmen of 1st

Platoon, Echo Company, 2d BN, 5th Marines: Ian Tawney, Zachary Harding, Vincent Osuna, Chad Kraus, Estevan Ponce, Brandon Teneyck, Anthony Labrum, Roberto Knapp, Kevin Thorsen, Baron Ochoa (Corpsman), Travis Johnson, Raphael Palisoc, Scott Kroner, Timothy Alexander, Christopher Smither, Geoffery Morrison, Carlos Medina, Trey Paus, Robert Nolan, Joel Klosterman, Joshua Brightman, Brandon Gathers, Sean Seaverns, Nathan Salvador, Christian Calderon, William Whitsett, Daniel Nelson, Nathan Gadson, Cody Hughes, Randy Stalcup, and Michael Medrano. Semper Fidelis.

I am forever grateful to the Marines of the Scout Sniper Platoon, H&S Company, 2d BN, 5th Marines: Daniel Bothwell, Ryan Coffman, Jacob Dolak, Kevin Frame, Jorge Garcia, Nathan Hervey, Steven Hoover, Jeffry Johnson, Jordan Laird, Raul Ponce, Juan Roblezalarcon, Corey Sherwood, Caleb Smith, Matt Smith, Logan Stark, Jarrod Tatom, Patrick Trujillo, and Mares Vega. Semper Fidelis.

The Marines of Task Force Southwest, 19-2: Eric Terashima, Patrick Joseph, Jason Browning, Josh Abraham, Hunter Davidhizar, James Tumolo, Parke Stevens, Kyle Himes, Stephen Heller, Anthony Sierawski, Jedidiah Thomas, Cody Leatherwood, Murphy Keefe, John Leahy, Mitchell Stuetelberg, Mallek Alqaryouti, Jeffery Carroll, and Patricia Clark.

Garth Massey and the Marines of Marine Corps Tactics and Operations Group (MCTOG) where I landed after a tumultuous sixteen months in Los Angeles. It was a pleasure serving with you. Semper Fidelis!

Tim Kudo, who makes a lot of things look easy and the difficult things effortless. Your friendship is one of the highlights of my time in the Marine Corps. Antoine Bates, I wish I had a fraction of your nonchalance. I've looked up to you ever since TBS and still do—Semper Fidelis! Owen Wrabel, you have a rare gift, share it with as many as possible. Jeremiah Flores, I'll never forget your encouragement, support, and generosity in San Juan Capistrano. Thank you and Semper Fidelis!

Ashley Tawney whose own strength and composure helped console me in the wake of Ian's death. Thank you for revisiting difficult memories and helping to fill in details, correct errors, and most of all for your continued friendship. Semper Fidelis! Don Roberts Jr., Caleb Giles, and Frank Denault—Semper Fidelis!

The family of Brian Christopher Grauman, thank you for taking my call several years ago and your willingness to listen to me and recall what I'm sure were exquisitely painful memories. I've dedicated this book to Brian's memory.

Bob Stephenson, Ken Connelly, and Jim Haase for leading by example.

Charles U. Daly and Charlie Daly, who were gracious enough to listen to my story and help allay my insecurities of publishing a book. *Sláinte!* I'm looking forward to our next 'micro-adventure.'

Chris Barber, whom I can trust to tell me the truth especially if it's uncomfortable and most especially if it involves breaking my balls. Semper Fidelis! Brian Raike and Greg Try who, years ago, read the very first draft of this book (if you could call it that). I'm gratified that you cared enough to read it in its unfinished and meandering clumsiness. Your feedback and perspective were invaluable.

Sarah Daly (no relation to father and son above), my homecoming from Afghanistan in 2020 was the COVID-19 pandemic. Your friendship, encouragement and incisive, candid feedback as I isolated myself to write this book were extremely helpful. With gratitude—thank you!

Craig Ferrario, whom I met as a fellow security guard at the W Hotel in Hollywood. Thank you for those real conversations at 3:00 a.m. about hard work, contentment, and gratitude as we ate a sandwich, chips, and a drink from Subway after our shifts. Your friendship, encouragement, and wisdom have been and still are invaluable to me. I hope you write your own story one day.

R.J. Beavers, who got me the job at the W Hotel when I had almost nothing. Thank you.

Jaline Perez, who without judgment or agenda, waited with me in a food line at Blessed Sacrament Food Pantry on Sunset Blvd. in Los Angeles. I'll never forget your kindness and generosity. Thank you.

Robert Delahunty, as I started writing, stopped, and began writing again, your encouragement, enthusiasm, and belief in this project *ab initio* have truly been gratifying. You encouraged me to press forward and trust my instinct that I had a story worth telling. (And you were the only one who could locate a fragment of a draft to remit to me after all work had been lost in Italy.) Your friendship, support, and wisdom have been an anchor in my life over the last fifteen years. Thank you.

My best friend Tom Alford, whether it be due to chance or Providence, our respective adventures we call 'life' have largely and miraculously remained in step since being stationed in California after law school. We have shared some of the best and worst experiences in life, which has been a lot of things, but thankfully not one of quiet desperation. I'm forever grateful for your companionship, intellect, and humor along the way and your encouragement to continue writing.

Major General Michael Fahey, Sergeant Major Carlton Kent, Major Tom Schueman, Nathaniel Fick, Jeremiah Workman, and Jake Edwards. The fact that I could call each of you for support in this endeavor and that you readily and enthusiastically rendered that support is the hallmark of *esprit de corps*. Thank you and Semper Fidelis!

Eliece Pool, Laura Cail, and the entire Scribe Media team. Thank you for helping make this book a reality.

Made in United States
North Haven, CT
08 February 2023

32220082R00146